*Exploring Shakespeare*

# A Midsummer Night's Dream

Approaches and activities

*Bernadette Fitzgerald*

Oxford University Press 1994

Oxford University Press, Walton Street, Oxford OX2 6DP

*Oxford New York Toronto*
*Delhi Bombay Calcutta Madras Karachi*
*Kuala Lumpur Singapore Hong Kong Tokyo*
*Nairobi Dar es Salaam Cape Town*
*Melbourne Auckland Madrid*

and associate companies in
*Berlin Ibadan*

*Oxford* is a trade mark of Oxford University Press

Introduction © Susan Leach 1994
Ways In, The Play and Overview © Bernadette Fitzgerald 1994

Published by Oxford University Press 1994

A CIP catalogue record for this book is available from the British Library

ISBN  0 19 831287 3

Printed in Great Britain at the University Press, Cambridge

## Acknowledgements

The cover illustration is by Anthea Toorchen.

The inside illustrations are by Jonathon Heap pp. 46, 92, 94; and Elitta Fell p. 59.

The publishers would like to thank the following for permission to reproduce
photographs:

The Bridgeman Art Library p. 34; Donald Cooper Photostage pp. 37 (both), 43
(right), 62 (left), 77 (left); Robbie Jack p. 30; Tristram Kenton pp. 43 (left), 62
(right), 77 (right), 80.

# Contents

# Introduction

## The *Exploring Shakespeare* series

These student study books to accompany *Romeo and Juliet*, *A Midsummer Night's Dream*, and *Julius Caesar* are intended primarily for Year 9 students working towards KS3 of the National Curriculum in English.

As they all offer a wide range of activities they can also be used with other secondary students, particularly those in years 10 and 11 working towards GCSE English and English (Literature).

The general purpose of the books is to enable the inexperienced student, probably coming to Shakespeare for the first time, to make sense of the plays from the start, and to find enjoyment in reading and working on them. We also hope that students' self-confidence in tackling Shakespeare will grow as a result of using these books, and that they will go on with enthusiasm to read and enjoy other plays by Shakespeare.

Each of the three books mirrors the individuality of its author, as well as reflecting a common approach to the study of the plays, based on active, collaborative work. The differences between the three books also reflect the very different natures of the three plays; however common the approach, each play demands its own separate treatment.

The books follow a common format:

1   An Introduction to Active Approaches, aimed at the teacher, which provides a simple explanation of the active approaches used across all three books; and a Ways In section, which offers students ideas for introductory work on the plays, before full study is begun. For students who already know the basic plot and characters, some of these suggestions will be redundant.

2   Activities on the play itself, scene by scene.

3   An Overview section, which offers activities to help students look back at the plays and consider them as complete entities, from a variety of viewpoints related to themes, imagery, language, characters, and plot.

The second section, of scene-by-scene activities on the play, requires a little more clarification. It has been organized so that usually more than one activity is offered for each scene. It is assumed that teachers will not work through these activities from start to finish, but will select assignments from the range on offer.

Scenes are prefaced by a brief resumé of their importance to the play, with an indication of their time and place. *Exploring Shakespeare: Romeo and Juliet* makes most obvious reference to time, with fewer specific references in *A Midsummer Night's Dream. Julius Caesar* is concerned with only a few salient calendar dates, and assumes the passing of time without mentioning it, so this has few specific references.

Where an activity refers to specific lines of text within a scene, a line reference is given, based on the *Oxford School Shakespeare* edition of the play.

Activities which require a cleared space for students to work in are marked in the text with an icon ▨. These activities are often the most challenging for the teacher to organize and oversee, so they may not be the first choice of teachers who are still 'finding their Shakespeare feet'!

Scene-by-scene activities are based on approaches designed to fulfil several purposes:
- to enable students to engage with the underlying concerns of the plays
- to encourage students to think for themselves, and be prepared to offer their own ideas and conclusions
- to help students work independently of direct supervision by the teacher, alone, in pairs, and in groups
- to take students into a deeper knowledge and understanding of the plays than is implied by the narrow requirements of KS3 SATs.

The activities suggested throughout the scene-by-scene pages include acting, improvisation, mime, freeze frames, and other use of voice and movement; written, visual/illustrative and stage/theatrical assignments; discussion, hotseating, and inquests; and searching and researching. The emphasis throughout is on taking on the language of the plays as it stands – on using its differences and challenges positively and creatively.

We suggest that students have a journal, log, or notebook for the written activities, especially for those which ask them to note down their thoughts or reactions. (Sometimes the word 'journal' is used in the students' books.)

These books can be used in different ways to fit in with students' previous experience. Where students have already read the play, or seen a film version of the play, the activities will help them explore the play in greater depth, and with help, consolidate what they already know. Where students are coming to the play for the first time, it is possible to run the student study book alongside the reading of the play. The preferred approach will need to be thought through by the teacher. Each way of using these students' books will produce different results and reactions in the classroom.

Assignments in the scene-by-scene sections make clear how students should be grouped, and sometimes suggest that they should get their teacher to help them. It has been taken for granted that teachers will set up each lesson, but the emphasis is always on students doing these assignments for themselves. They are consistently addressed as 'you' in active collaboration with each other.

## Introduction to active approaches

Many of the active approaches used in these books are already well-established as good classroom practice, while others are based on techniques developed by theatre practitioners.

### Reading

Because students coming new to Shakespeare are unfamiliar with Shakespeare's language and verse form, it is useful to have a range of reading techniques at hand to help them grasp the meaning of the texts. The reading techniques described below emphasize particular features of different kinds of text. All the techniques can be used with pairs, groups, or whole classes. They are designed to involve all students in reading. Success with these techniques depends on all students using the same edition of the play, because of variations in punctuation between editions.

It is advisable to try out all these reading techniques with a class, so that students know how to use them when working independently.

### Reading by punctuation marks

Have students seated in a large circle if possible. They read in turns round the group, each person stopping and handing on to the next person at a punctuation mark.

Reading by punctuation marks makes long speeches in blank verse manageable for students, and helps them grasp the ideas and development of thought in a speech. The words between punctuation marks express one idea or thought, even the word 'and': every speech moves from an opening statement, question, or proposition to another position. The technique highlights single words and images, and helps students identify metaphor and imagery. Many assignments which ask students to find key words and images, thoughts and feelings in the text depend on this reading technique.

Where students are using this technique in a pair or a small group, the same method applies.

Reading by 'sense units' (usually marked off by full stops, semicolons or the word 'and') is a variation of this. It invites students to ignore commas and read on until there is a sense 'pause', rather than having maybe only a single word to read.

### Reading by sentences

This technique allows whole thoughts to be read/heard at once. The irregularity of sentence length in speeches and the linking of thoughts are clearly shown by using this method. A development of this is to write out each sentence separately to see how the thinking has moved on from one idea to the next. Some assignments build on this by asking students to headline the main thought in a sentence.

### Reading by speeches

Many scenes in the plays work best with one person reading the whole of any speech, and the next person reading the next speech, and so on round the group. This retains whole group involvement, without burdening individuals with the responsibility for 'parts'. It allows the cohesion of each character's words to be taken in, and is a good technique to use when whole scenes are being read in which no character speaks more than about six lines at once.

A mixture of all techniques can be used in any speech or scene; it is a good idea to vary these approaches when working on any part of the plays.

### Classroom organization

All these techniques can be used in the classroom, by students sitting at desks or at groups of desks. This is not ideal, but at least all are participating and experiencing the text. The focus here would be on reading and listening.

A space allowing students to sit in a circle encourages more collaborative participation: it focuses attention on the text and on each student in turn, and emphasizes the importance of each individual's contribution.

A space allowing physical movement offers the greatest possibilities. Physicalizing techniques can be used here, marrying physical movement with one or more reading techniques.

## Physical work

The following suggestions for physical ways of working on the plays are not all explicitly included in the activities in the book. They are offered here, in outline, for the teacher who may wish to go beyond static reading of the texts, but who does not want students to 'act it out' yet. In all of them, it is assumed that the teacher will be working with a whole class, or large group. The use of the reading techniques described above is implied in these physical activities.

By involving physical movement, these techniques:

- make clear that this is the language of theatre, to be spoken out loud
- release the potential energy of the words, and allow students to experience the power of the language.

## Moving to the words

- Students walk, or run, round the room, reading the chosen piece of text aloud all together. They change direction at every punctuation point, or every sentence, or every end of line. Choose a speed and type of movement to help students experience the energy and rhythms of the verse.

- The teacher, facing the students standing in their own space in the room, reads the lines aloud, divided into 'sense units'; students repeat the words, and 'show' their meaning at the same time. For example, as they repeat the words, 'Gallop apace, you fiery-footed steeds, towards Phoebus' lodging', for the first time, students might be expected to gallop, to indicate 'fiery steeds' in their movement, and to be puzzled by 'Phoebus' lodging'. Briefly explain 'Phoebus' lodging' and ask them to try again.

  Assignments which ask students to visualize and illustrate images and meaning can be started off with this method.

- Set up physical impediments to the readers. The idea is not to create chaos, but to 'challenge' readers into vocalizing the emotion and energy in the words. In several of these methods, students can be given a line to learn before the activity takes place, so they are not hampered by books as they move about. Some methods are:
  a  crowd in round one person reading the chosen speech, echoing key words pre-selected by the teacher
  b  make pairs pull against each other as they read a speech between them
  c  make one reader of the selected speech do some physical task, for example stacking books, moving from one chair to another on punctuation points
  d  allocate lines to groups at each end of the room; in order of the lines, students run across the room shouting out their words
  e  one person reads; one or more students try to stop him or her crossing the room.

## More active reading

- Use the chosen reading approach round the circle; each speaker turns to face the next to say their words.

- Use the chosen reading approach round the circle: each reader walks to the middle of the circle to say their words, if possible with an appropriate gesture to show their meaning.

- As one group of students reads the lines, other students are asked to echo and repeat key words and ideas.

- Vary the pace of any physical activity.

- Vary the volume in reading activities – ask students to use their voice control to whisper, shout, and make appropriate vocal sound effects.

- Work on the words in the verse whose meaning is entirely dependent on context, for example 'here', 'you', 'me', 'that', 'he', 'her', 'she'. These are known as *deictic* words.

Two people reading Paris's and Juliet's interchange –

Paris:    Do not deny to *him* that *you* love *me*.
Juliet:   *I* will confess to *you* that *I* love *him*.

– highlight these deictic words by pointing to themselves on 'I' and 'me', the other person on 'you', and at Friar Laurence (or an agreed spot in the room) on 'him'. Focusing like this on these words makes their meaning absolutely clear in the specific context. For more complex speeches or interchanges, involving reference to more than one other person, the room can be prepared by pinning up round the walls the names of these characters. As students read, they point to the relevant name, or themselves, on each deictic word. 'Here', 'there', 'up', 'down' and so on can also be treated in this way.

This treatment of deictic words will work whichever reading method has been chosen.

## Further active approaches

Additional techniques can be used to increase students' knowledge and understanding of the text.

### *Acting/presentation*

Some activities ask students to act out a scene or part of a scene. This is very useful for students with the confidence to do it, but for others a joint presentation can be preferable.

By using a combination of different reading and physical techniques, students can prepare presentations which involve everyone, without inhibiting those who dislike being 'on show' on their own. One example: in each group some students can be responsible for reading one part between them, while other students work out mimes to accompany the spoken words.

### Mime

Mime is useful for students who have yet to gain the confidence to read aloud. It can be developed into 'dumbshow', a mimed presentation of the main action of a scene, or to show the actions of characters as described by others: for example, when Puck describes the flight of the Athenian workmen after Bottom appears with the ass's head; when Benvolio describes two of the street fights; when Casca describes Caesar being offered the crown.

### Hotseating, interviewing, interrogating

In each of these activities, a student takes on the role of a character in the play and is questioned about that character's actions, motivation, and thoughts.

In **hotseating**, the whole class or group questions the character. This allows all students to become involved, although they may not all wish to participate.

In **interviewing**, a group or pair, with a specific purpose in mind (producing a newspaper report, television interview, radio interview, other write-up) interviews one person (or each other) in role as a character. Here, each person has a clearly defined part to play.

In **interrogation**, which can be done in groups or pairs, a student in role is put under duress, as in a real interrogation, about their part in the play. Good candidates for this treatment are Brutus, Cassius, and the Tribunes in *Julius Caesar*, Friar Laurence in *Romeo and Juliet*, Puck and Oberon in *A Midsummer Night's Dream*.

### Inquest, court hearing

These are more formal frameworks for use when questioning characters, and are described fully where they occur in the activities on the play itself (pages 19–67).

## Improvisation

Some assignments ask students to improvise
- the moments before a scene starts
- a similar situation to the one shown in a scene
- action described by a character but not seen on stage.

This can be linked to:

## Freeze frames

(This is also know as tableaux, still photographs, or still images.)
In this method, students produce a static representation
designed to reveal the deeper meanings and significance of
- a moment in a scene
- the relationship between a group of characters
- what a character imagines
- images in the text.

Where it is used to represent a moment from a scene, students
can be asked to explain the thoughts and feelings of their
character, and the motivation behind their frozen stance at that
very moment.

## Other activities

In addition to active reading techniques and physical activities,
the assignments included in this book offer a wide range of other
tasks intended to encourage and maintain the students'
engagement with the text.

These task are all described where they occur in the activities on
the play (pages 19–67), and include:

### Written assignments

Students are invited to produce a wide range of written
responses to the texts. These are well-established in current
classroom practice (many of them can be found listed at the end
of the original Cox Report) and include letters, diaries, point-of-
view writing, accounts of events, students' own playscripts,
letters to and from an agony aunt, newspaper headlines, front
page reports and articles, stream-of-consciousness writing,
dossiers on characters, and obituaries.

## Activities based on the play as theatre

Students are asked in some assignments to think about a part of the text as a piece to be staged, reminding them that the texts are above all plays for the theatre.

Students are invited to:

- design the stage set and costumes for a particular scene
- produce sound effects and tape them
- take the director's role, and make decisions about cutting, moving, or changing scenes or parts of scenes
- annotate a script with stage directions for the actors.

## Text-based activities

These encourage students to look very closely at the text to:

- select single quotations which sum up whole speeches
- search through an act or the whole play for key images
- present a 'bare bones' or five-minute version of the play by stripping it down to essentials, still using the language of the play.

## Showing and sharing

Finally, when students have completed an assignment, they are sometimes invited to share their work with other groups or with the whole class. When the work is active, requiring space and time, thought needs to be given to setting up the classroom for this, and to building in time for reflection, response, and reaction.

## Ways in

## Characters – who's who?

These activities will help you if you know nothing about the play yet. Make a large name label (self-adhesive labels are useful here, or use card and sellotape) for each of the characters in the play, repeating names where needed up to the number of students in the class. Each student takes one label and wears it so all can see it. The whole class stands in a spread-out circle.

First, to become familiar with the sound of the names:

- go round the circle, saying the name of your character
- go round the circle again, saying your name in a voice which you think goes with the character.

Then play these two games.

### 'Jack to Jill'

*Swap places*

In this game, people take it in turns to choose someone else in the circle and cross over to them, saying their own name and the name of the person they have chosen: for example 'Egeus to Peaseblossom'. When 'Egeus' gets to 'Peaseblossom', Peaseblossom must continue by crossing to someone else, saying (for example) 'Peaseblossom to Helena'. The game continues until all characters have said their names, and crossed the circle. You can make this much more fun by doing it at top speed!

[If you don't yet know each other very well in the class, this is a good game to play with your own names before you do anything else. It will help you work together later on.]

### Categories

To learn more about the characters, get your teacher to help you with this game. Stay in the circle with your name labels on. Get your teacher to go round behind the circle, sticking a label on your back which describes you as a ruler/courtier, a young lover, a fairy, or a workman. Your teacher does not tell you which label you have been given but the words are then written on the board so you know what they all are.

When you all have your labels, you move round the room to find and join up with the other members of your group. You are allowed to ask each person you meet only one question: 'Am I a — (ruler/courtier, lover, fairy, workman)?' If someone asks you this question, you can only answer 'Yes' or 'No', after you've looked at their label. When you have found out who you are, find the rest of your group by asking people, 'Are you a — (ruler/courtier, lover, fairy, workman)?' When all the groups are complete it is time for the next activity.

### Freeze frames 1: harmony

In your group – rulers/courtiers, lovers, fairies, workmen – work out a freeze frame to show how your group would look in a photograph taken on a special occasion, like a wedding. Decide whether they are looking at the camera, or at other people in the group. Then put all the freeze frames together, for one big photograph, showing how you think the groups would fit together.

You could invite another teacher or student into your classroom to see if they can work out from your big freeze frame which kind of character each of you is.

### *Freeze frames 2: disagreement*

Working with your own group, make up another freeze frame, this time showing your group in an unguarded moment, when some disagreement is going on. For now, make up your own disagreements. Later on, you will discover what they are in the play itself.

## Magic and illusion

There is a lot of magic in this play, sometimes used for good purposes, sometimes for bad.

Divide the class into four groups, each choosing one of these spells to work on:

> Oberon:  Flower of this purple dye,
> Hit with Cupid's archery,
> Sink in apple of his eye.
> When his love he doth espy,
> Let her shine as gloriously
> As the Venus of the sky.
> When thou wak'st, if she be by,
> Beg of her for remedy.

> Oberon:  What thou seest when thou dost wake,
> Do it for thy true-love take;
> Love and languish for his sake.
> Be it ounce, or cat, or bear,
> Pard, or boar with bristled hair,
> In thy eye that shall appear
> When thou wak'st, it is thy dear.
> Wake when some vile thing is near.

> Puck:  On the ground,
> Sleep sound:
> I'll apply
> To your eye,

> Gentle lover, remedy.
> When thou wak'st,
> Thou tak'st
> True delight
> In the sight
> Of thy former lady's eye:
> And the country proverb known,
> That every man should take his own,
> In your waking shall be shown:
> Jack shall have Jill;
> Naught shall go ill;
> The man shall have his mare again,
> And all shall be well.

Puck:
> Churl, upon thy eyes I throw
> All the power this charm doth owe.
> When thou wak'st, let love forbid
> Sleep his seat on thy eyelid:
> So awake when I am gone,
> For I must now to Oberon.

The spells are all to do with putting something on the eyes of a sleeping person.

In your group:

■   read the lines of your spell round the group
■   decide if it is a 'good' or a 'bad' spell
■   work out what it is supposed to do
■   act it out, having one person on the ground as the sleeper, the rest of the group sharing out the lines, and all going up to the sleeper to put the spell on their eyes.

As a class, watch each other's little performances, and then discuss your ideas so far about the speakers of these spells.

As a class, see if you can work out which spell comes first in the play, and which comes last.

## Illusion

Work in the same groups. As quickly as you can, note down together your ideas about illusions. What are they? How are they created? For example, films and television present the illusion of real people and places, but if you touch them there's only a screen there. The illusion is created by projecting light through celluloid, or changing electrical signals into visual images on the TV screen.

To get started, you could think about:

- ghosts
- shadow puppets
- make-up and masks
- 'virtual reality'.

Bring all your ideas together as a class. Divide them into two lists: illusions that can only be created using equipment, and illusions that depend on other things.

Look back at the spells you worked on earlier. What was used to create the illusions? What were the illusions?

## Tragic young lovers: Pyramus and Thisbe

Young lovers with problems are a key theme in *A Midsummer Night's Dream*. As a class, read this short version of the old story of Pyramus and Thisbe.

Pyramus was a young man of Babylon who fell in love with Thisbe. Their parents forbade them to marry but the two lovers exchanged vows through a chink in the wall which separated their two houses. They agreed to meet at the tomb of Ninus, outside the walls of Babylon, under a white mulberry tree. Thisbe was the first to arrive but, being frightened by a lioness, she fled into a cave, dropping her veil to the ground as she ran. The lioness covered it in blood. When Pyramus arrived he found the bloody veil and, convinced that Thisbe had been killed and devoured, he stabbed himself with his sword. Thisbe, emerging from the cave and distraught at the sight of the dying Pyramus, fell upon his sword.

### Characters

In groups, take one of the following parts each: Pyramus, Thisbe, Thisbe's mother, Thisbe's father, a lion, a wall, Pyramus' father, Pyramus' mother.

## Presentation

Make up your own play version of the story. You could include the following scenes:

- Pyramus and Thisbe meet for the first time
- Pyramus argues with his parents
- Thisbe argues with her parents
- Pyramus and Thisbe speak through a hole in a wall
- their tragic deaths.

You may choose a member of your group to direct your rehearsal. Prepare your play and present it to the rest of your class.

Now, in your group you may choose to read the play version of this story in *A Midsummer Night's Dream* (Act 5 scene 1 lines 126–335).

You will notice that the play is interrupted by other characters, and that the cast of characters is slightly different from yours.

As a class, discuss the differences between the play you made up, and the play presented by the Athenian workmen. Which did you prefer? Do you think the play is a good one to present at someone's wedding celebration? Discuss your opinions.

# The play

## Act 1 scene 1

*The day before Midsummer's Night. Theseus' Palace, Athens. Theseus and Hippolyta are eagerly looking forward to their wedding day. They are interrupted by Egeus who accuses Lysander of having stolen his daughter Hermia's heart, making her unwilling to marry Demetrius, the man whom Egeus has chosen for her.*

### Love and marriage

The scene introduces the theme of love and marriage from different viewpoints:

- Theseus and Hippolyta, who are to be married in four days' time
- Hermia, whose father Egeus has arranged a marriage for her with Demetrius
- Lysander, who has wooed Hermia and wants to marry her for love. She returns his love
- Demetrius, who once loved another woman, Helena, but now wants to marry Hermia.

In pairs, produce:

*either* a notice containing news of the wedding of Theseus and Hippolyta, to be attached to the palace gate for the benefit of citizens who did not hear the announcement which Philostrate might have made;

*or* an advertisement inviting people to put in proposals for entertainments for Theseus' wedding.

 ### Theseus and Hippolyta                    *lines 1–19*

Work with a partner, and note down anything unusual you find about the way Theseus wooed Hippolyta.

Draw a sketch (stick people will do), or work out a freeze frame to show Theseus wooing Hippolyta. Write a short caption underneath your sketch to sum it up, using Theseus' words.

 ### Egeus and Hermia                                    *lines 26–38*

Egeus describes how he thinks Lysander wooed Hermia. Look at his words and draw a sketch or work out a freeze frame to show Lysander wooing Hermia. Add a short caption to sum up what happened, using Egeus' words.

Write down the differences you noticed between these two kinds of wooing. Which would you prefer?

 ### Full of vexation                                    *lines 22–45*

Egeus is very angry. He ends his opening speech by asking for the law of Athens to be used against his daughter, to support him. But what is he so angry about? To find out, read his words in this way:

Have the names 'Lysander', 'Demetrius', 'Hermia', and 'Theseus' pinned up round the classroom. Share the reading of lines 22–45 round the class, standing in a big circle and reading in turn by sense units (usually finishing with a comma or a full stop). If your words refer to any of the four names, point to the correct one (or ones) with a very big, dramatic gesture. If your words refer to Egeus point to yourself with a big gesture. Words which show this are 'me', 'my', 'mine', 'I'.

Do this again, making Egeus sound angry and shouting out his words.

With your partner, discuss and note down:
■ your opinion of the law of Athens as it supports fathers
■ three statements in support of Egeus
■ three statements against Egeus.

Use your ideas in a whole class discussion about Egeus' treatment of Hermia.

## Theseus and Hermia                                *lines 46–90*

With your partner, look at the conversation between Theseus
and Hermia. What is he trying to make her do? Pick out his most
threatening statements, and note them down.

 Join with another pair to work on his statement at line 47:

> 'To you, your father should be as a god'.

Does this strike you as a good way of looking at a father? Discuss
your ideas about fathers and their relationships with their
children, and then make up two freeze frames: one to show
Theseus' words in operation, and one to show your own ideas
about fathers.

Now, imagine that you are Hermia and write down her reactions
to being told that she must do as her father commands.

## Choices                                          *lines 65–78*

What would you do in Hermia's place? Look at Theseus' and
Hermia's words. The three options offered by Theseus are
1   marry Demetrius
2   die
3   live in a convent, as a nun.

Work in groups of three or four. Read lines 65–78, in sense units,
round the group.

Try reading the lines in two different ways:
■   as if Theseus feels sorry for Hermia
■   as if he is trying to scare and shock her.

Discuss which of the two different ways of reading you preferred.
How do you, as a modern reader, react to the choices which
Hermia is offered?

Then discuss:
■   what might happen to Hermia if this play were a tragedy
    instead of a comedy
■   what might happen to Hermia if this were a modern play or
    soap opera (like *EastEnders*).

Which of the three choices seems worst to you? (To live as a nun in a convent means dedicating your life and soul to God, never seeing any men, and dying without ever having children.) Which one would you choose? Note down your thoughts, and your reasons.

 ### Convent life                                          *lines 65–90*

In pairs, pick out the words and phrases which Theseus uses to make convent life seem hard – a big sacrifice. Present a freeze frame to the class to illustrate two of his words or phrases.

### Violence                                                    *lines 1–90*

Up to this point in the scene, violence has been described or threatened several times: note down the lines (and their speakers) where this happened. What would you say the balance is so far between violence and love? Think about this and note down your opinions.

### Demetrius and Lysander                         *lines 91–110*

These lines sketch in the beginnings of the rivalry between these two men. Lysander shows Demetrius in a bad light. Look at the table below:

| Past | Present |
| --- | --- |
| Demetrius loved Helena | Demetrius now loves Hermia not Helena but |
| Helena loved Demetrius | Helena still loves Demetrius |

What can have made Demetrius change?

**Theseus and Demetrius**                          *lines 111–114*

In pairs, imagine that Theseus talks to Demetrius after they leave
the stage about his fickle treatment of the doting Helena, and
about why he insists on marrying Hermia, who does not love
him. Improvise the conversation they might have had. Include a
reason why Theseus has not spoken to Demetrius sooner about
his treatment of Helena.

When you are happy with your improvisation, write down their
conversation.

 **'Come, my Hippolyta; what cheer, my love?'**  *line 122*

What makes Theseus ask Hippolyta this question? What look
does he see on her face? Throughout the passionate arguments,
Hippolyta has not spoken.

Discuss in pairs and write down:
- why you think that she has not spoken
- what she was thinking and doing while the debate raged
- whom she might have sympathized with.

In pairs, improvise then write the conversation which she and
Theseus have when they are alone. Consider how she might feel
and speak about Hermia's situation and the way Theseus dealt
with it.

**'The course of true love . . .'**                     *lines 128–155*

For the first time in the play, Hermia and Lysander are left alone
together. In pairs, read Lysander's expressions of misery and
Hermia's comments on them (lines 135–140).

Pick out, mime, and write down key words which they use to
describe their idea of the suffering associated with true love.

There are exclamation marks after Hermia's opening words in
lines 136, 138, and 140. Say these words aloud in a way which
shows how she feels.

Produce a spider graph or chart to illustrate the reasons why the course of true love never runs smoothly. Lines 135–149 will help you.

| Forces threatening true love | line | Quotation |
|---|---|---|
| social class | 135 | 'different in blood' |

### Lysander's plan                                         *lines 150–168*

Whilst Hermia recommends that they must be patient (line 152), Lysander suggests a plan of action – that they elope! As a class, read aloud Lysander's plan (lines 156–168) in different ways: anxiously, excitedly, firmly. Decide which way of reading worked best.

Write down what you think Lysander's and Hermia's reactions to their situation show about their characters.

### Lysander's letter

Write the letter which Lysander could have written to his aunt. When planning the letter, consider what he would tell her about:

- why he is asking his aunt for help
- Hermia's dangerous situation
- her father's attitude to him
- the risks they are taking by eloping, especially the risks Hermia runs
- his feelings for Hermia.

### How to swear!                                    *lines 169–178*

With a partner, read Hermia's extended oaths which she uses to persuade Lysander of her sincerity (lines 164–178). Now, re-read these lines, varying the loudness of your voice, your tones of voice (for example speaking firmly, despairingly), your facial expressions and body language. You could also try different ways of emphasizing key words or images. Show your interpretation to another pair and watch their version. Discuss the differences you noticed.

### Hermia and Helena                                *lines 180–225*

In threes, read the dialogue between Helena, Hermia, and Lysander. Experiment with different ways of reading Hermia's and Helena's lines, for example in a friendly way, sadly, angrily . . .

Both Helena and Hermia are facing problems at this stage. In your journal, sum up:

- Hermia's problems
- Helena's problems
- the different ways in which they react to their problems.

### Problem page                                     *lines 181–245*

Write Helena's letter to an agony aunt explaining her problems and seeking advice. (Look closely at the text for ideas, e.g. lines 181–193 in which Helena describes all the qualities of Hermia which she envies and would like to have to help her to attract Demetrius.) Include how Helena feels about Demetrius, and how he has reacted to her. (You will find details of Demetrius' behaviour in lines 226–245.)

Then write the agony aunt's letter of reply. What advice would she give Helena?

### What is love?                                    *lines 226–251*

As a class, taking a line each, read lines 226–251. These lines include Helena's definition of love. What does she think love is? Do you agree with her? As a class, discuss Helena's ideas, then working on your own write in any style you choose a piece entitled 'Love is . . .'. How many ideas about love have been mentioned in the play so far? Include in your writing as many as you can.

### Helena's plan                                         *lines 246–251*

Write down:

■  what Helena plans to do
■  her state of mind as she decides to betray her best friend
■  the imaginary conversation in which Helena tells Demetrius of Hermia's plan to elope. Write the conversation so that the reader will sympathize with Helena.

### Diary

Write a detailed diary entry for Hermia, Lysander, or Helena at the end of Act 1 scene 1.

## Act 1 scene 2

*The same day. Peter Quince's house in Athens.*
*Scene 2 moves from the aristocratic characters to ordinary Athenian workmen, known as the 'Mechanicals'. As a result of Theseus' request for 'merriments' on his wedding day (Act 1 scene 1 lines 11–15), six workmen meet to cast and produce a play in his honour. This scene introduces humour which runs through the play.*

### Production problems

The play to be acted by Bottom and the other Mechanicals is about love. Later, you find out how much the story of their play parallels the situation of Hermia and Lysander.

For the meantime, the little company of amateur actors has genuine problems concerning how to present their play. Peter Quince, who is the director, has cast it beforehand.

Work in groups. After you have read through the scene in parts, make a cast list for the play, with its full title. Then note down all the problems mentioned by the characters. For example: what wig to wear, what voice to speak in.

This scene illustrates what hard work comedy is: being funny takes a lot of rehearsal!

 ### Creating a character

Look carefully at the words spoken by the character whose part you read. Write down a short description that sums him up.

Then think about how you can show what sort of person he is by the way you read and act out his lines. Try to work out his:

- facial expressions
- pitch and volume of voice
- speed of delivering a line
- use of an accent – which one?
- body movements and mannerisms (ways of walking, hiccuping, etc.).

This will help you to create a real personality for your character.

It may help to work in pairs on this part of the activity, so that your partner can tell you whether your ideas for presenting your character work.

Finally, re-read and act the scene in your group, trying to include all your ideas in your performance.

### Humour: amateur dramatics                    *lines 1–104*

The Mechanicals do their best; they are not trying to be funny, but . . .

In pairs, pick out the different ways in which humour is the result of their serious attempts, and write down examples. Here are some ideas to get you started:

- contradictions, for example 'wedding day at night'
- Bottom's constant interruptions – and the reasons for them
- Bottom's exaggerated reading of poetic lines (lines 27–34)
- Flute's reluctance to play a woman's part
- Snug's comments about his lion's part.

### Newspaper interview

Imagine that the *Athens Observer* has found out that Peter Quince is rehearsing a play for Theseus' wedding. After the others go home, a reporter knocks on his door, and interviews him about progress so far. Write the interview that takes place.

### Act 1 revisited

Divide the class into six groups. Each group chooses one of the main characters in Act 1: Theseus, Egeus, Hermia, Lysander, Demetrius, Helena.

Look back over the words spoken by your character, and choose up to six lines which reveal the most important things about him or her. Write your chosen lines out on big sheets of paper, and have them ready for your next activity.

Devise two freeze frames to illustrate just *two* of your lines. When it is your group's turn, pin up your sheet of paper, and show your freeze frames to the class. The class guesses which two lines your freeze frames are illustrating.

### What happens next?

In your notes, predict:
- what you think could happen to the four young lovers
- what you expect to happen when the Mechanicals next meet 'at the Duke's Oak'.

### Act 1: in and out of love

Draw a diagram to show whom each of the following characters loves at the end of Act 1: Lysander, Helena, Hermia, Demetrius. Keep your diagram safe – you will need to refer to it later.

## Act 2 scene 1

*The next night, Midsummer Night. A wood near Athens. This scene moves into another world – 'Fairyland', a magical and strange world. We are introduced to the mischievous Puck and learn about his magical pranks. Events in the fairy world echo the concerns of the human world. Oberon and Titania, the king and queen of the fairies, are in the middle of a furious quarrel.*

## A magical world

> **fairy** (n) a small imaginary being with magical powers
> **fairyland** (n) the imaginary home of fairies; an enchanted region
>
> *Concise Oxford Dictionary*

In Shakespeare's day, many people believed in magical, supernatural beings such as goblins and fairies. The supernatural beings in this play have certain powers, but they are also creatures of the night, and have to disappear at daybreak. Puck was also known as Robin Goodfellow: people believed in him as a household spirit, who could help as well as hinder you.

Shakespeare obviously had to use ordinary people as actors for the fairy parts in the play. But, as well as having magic powers, the fairies in *A Midsummer Night's Dream* are meant to be small and invisible to the human characters. The way Shakespeare solved this problem was by his use of language: as you read the fairy scenes, watch out for words and phrases which indicate a very small scale of things, and places where the fairies are invisible to the humans.

 ### 'I am that merry wanderer of the night' *lines 32–57*

In small groups, read lines 32–57, and select three of the pranks which Puck boasts that he enjoys playing on mortals. Create mimes to show what each prank involves. While some of your group present the mimes, others read the relevant lines from the text to accompany the mime.

In your groups, discuss any differences you have spotted between Puck and a normal human being.

### 'Oberon is passing fell and wrath'

*lines 20–31,
60–145*

As a whole class, divide into pairs to read Puck's explanation of why Oberon is so angry with Titania (lines 20–31). Each pair reads a line. Briefly give your opinion of whether he is justified in being so angry.

There is a serious rift between Oberon and Titania over the changeling child. She is refusing to have anything to do with Oberon, and he is trying to reassert his authority over her.

In pairs, look at lines 64–80, and decide what they are accusing each other of and why Titania won't give up the child.

Then look at Titania's speech, lines 81–117. She describes Oberon's jealous behaviour, and the effect of their warring on the natural world of the human beings. Find lines which match these statements:

- Titania's revels are ruined by Oberon
- the rivers are overflowing
- the crops won't grow
- the flocks of sheep are dead
- there is mud everywhere
- life is miserable for humans
- it is winter when it should be summer
- in winter, summer flowers come out
- the seasons are in a mess.

What does she mean when she says lines 115–117?
What reply is she hoping for from Oberon?
What reply does she get?

As a class, read Titania's speech, changing readers at punctuation marks, and making her words sound angry or sad to bring out her feelings.

### 'Not for thy fairy kingdom'

The royal couple do not resolve their problems here.

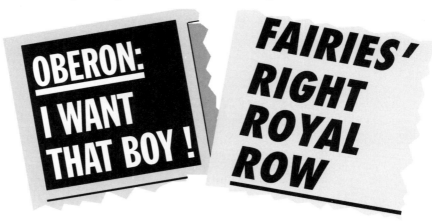

Divide the class into groups. Each group writes one of the following front-page newspaper articles:

- the argument from Titania's point of view, justifying her actions and criticizing Oberon: look at lines 121–145 for help
- the argument from Oberon's point of view, mentioning his view that a wife should obey her husband: look at lines 60–143.

Think carefully about eye-catching headlines and sub-headlines. Will you also include drawings or photographs?

Like other male characters in the play, Oberon wants to get his own way: which other characters can you think of, who behave in the same way?

## Love-in-idleness                                    *lines 146–187*

Because he cannot get what he wants, Oberon plots his revenge on Titania. He decides to use the magic properties of a flower. How did he know about this little western flower, and the power of its juice?

Look at his story of what happened when he was once sitting on a promontory, and heard a mermaid singing. With a partner tell the story in your own words of what happened to change this harmless little flower into a powerful love potion. Then complete this grid:

| |
| --- |
| *Name of flower:* |
| *Colour:* |
| *Appearance:* |
| *Where found:* |
| *Powers of juice:* |
| *Antidote:* |
| *Plant changed by:* |
| *How to apply:* |

With a partner, discuss your opinion of Oberon's intentions in lines 177–185. Would you call his intentions revenge or something else?

Because Oberon then watches (invisibly) Demetrius and Helena, and takes pity on Helena, he decides to use the flower to do some good – as he thinks.

### Helena and Demetrius argue                         *lines 188–224*

In pairs, read Demetrius and Helena's argument (lines 188–244). Discuss how they feel towards each other. Choose three or four lines which show the strength of their emotions about their situation – Helena's obsessive love for Demetrius, and his loathing of her – and write them down. Make a note of how you react to Helena when she says, 'Use me but as your spaniel . . .' (line 205). How would you describe this type of love?

 ### Demetrius' threats

How serious are Demetrius' threats? Work in groups to hotseat one person as Helena and one as Demetrius. The group can ask questions about your fears and intentions in the wood.

If you are Helena, do you really believe that you are in any danger from Demetrius?

If you are Demetrius, do you really intend to hurt Helena?

### I know a bank                                       *lines 249–256*

Look at Oberon's speech carefully to give yourself an idea of the scale, or size of things, that he is talking about. You might also see how many of the flowers he mentions that you know or have heard of. If Titania sleeps on this bank, do you think this suggests she is very small?

### The first cock crow                                 *line 267*

Oberon emphasizes how quickly things must be done to fit into the short Midsummer Night: the tasks so far are to put the juice on Titania's eyes, and to put juice on the eyes of 'an Athenian youth'.

This painting shows a Victorian artist's idea of the size of Titania, Oberon, and the fairies. Does this match your impression of them, from what you have read of the play so far?

 ## In the hot seat!

Work in groups of five or six. Sit in a circle and elect one person to sit in the middle, as Oberon. The rest of you should question Oberon thoroughly about his feelings and plans at this point. Your questions could include:

- What did you think of Demetrius' behaviour towards Helena?
- Why did you decide to help Helena?
- What do you intend to do with the flower?
- What do you hope will happen to your victim?
- What will happen to anyone who has the juice on his or her eyes?

- How do you feel towards Titania at this point?
- What job did you give to Puck? What information did you give him to help him find his victim? Do you have any doubts about his ability to do the job properly?
- How would you describe your motives as you plan to use the flower juice yourself, and instruct Puck to intervene in the mortal world in the relationship between Helena and Demetrius?

Can you think of any other questions to ask Oberon?

Using the information and ideas you have just gathered to help you, write an 'interior monologue' – in other words, Oberon's private thoughts – at this point in the play.

### The fairy world

What have you noticed so far about the three fairy characters, Oberon, Titania, and Puck? Before you look at the next scene, discuss with your partner what words you would use to label them. For example: good-natured, pleasant, friendly, aggressive, fun-loving, mischievous, spiteful, vengeful, greedy, selfish, sweet, pretty, welcoming? Any of these, or none of them? Think of your own ideas too and note them down. Remember them as you read on.

## Act 2 scene 2

*The same night. Another part of the wood.*
*In this scene, things change when the magic flower juice is squeezed onto Titania's eyes and, mistakenly, onto Lysander's eyes. As a result of this, there are far-reaching comic and chaotic consequences: order will not be completely restored until the end of Act 4.*

### Enter Titania, with her attendants          *lines 1–30*

With your partner, look at lines 1–8, and note down the things Titania mentions. Notice how fast things must happen: 'the third part of a minute.'

### Enjoy yourselves with the fairies' song!

In a circle, read the song through round the class, a line each (some lines may have to be said more than once to give each person a turn).

Allocate two or three lines to each pair. Work out the best way you can to say your lines: remember, this is a lullaby to lull Titania to sleep; you are warning harmful creatures away from her. Use echoing, repetition, whispering, and voice sounds to go with the words (for example, hissing for the snakes). When you have practised your lines, say the lullaby round the circle in the right sequence. You may want to practise this more than once to make it really good. Some people might feel confident enough to hum, or even sing their words!

### The wood

As a class, discuss the impressions of the wood which you gain from lines 1–32. Think about:
- the creatures which the fairies refer to in their lullaby
- the atmosphere which is created by these lines
- the implication of line 32, 'one aloof stand sentinel'.

### Wake when some vile thing is near          *lines 33–40*

Work as a class on these lines to show clearly what Oberon intends to do to humiliate Titania.

Choose one of the class to be Titania and lie on the floor asleep in the middle of the circle formed by the rest of the class.

Take one line each, round the class, repeating lines so that everyone has a line. When it's your turn, go up to Titania as you say your line, mime the action of squeezing the juice on her eyes, and say your line in a way to suit its meaning. When everyone has said their line, ask Titania what it felt like!

Discuss what you feel about Oberon's attitude to Titania in these lines.

### Oberon's thoughts

Puck does not hear him say these lines, nor has he seen Oberon cast his spell. In pairs, write what Oberon could have said to Puck as he

■ boasts about what he has just done to Titania
■ explains how he feels about Titania at this point
■ justifies his actions.

### Magical characters on stage

In small groups, discuss how the fairy characters are presented in the two photographs from past productions of the play. Which presentation do you prefer? Say why.

This is a good point to think about the problems of staging: how to represent fairies on stage, and make them look different from the humans.

Creating the fairy characters and the wood which they inhabit, on stage, is a challenge for costume and set designers. Over the centuries, the fairies have been presented in various different ways, for example:

- as if in a ballet, in gauze tutus – looking romantic and pretty
- as children (apart from Oberon and Titania) – looking sweet and whimsical
- adults covered in gold paint – looking stylized and symbolic
- feathered and birdlike – looking strange and surreal
- as puppets, operated by actors dressed in black, with clever use of lighting.

The designer of a production needs to know what ideas the director has. Imagine the director of a production wishes to experiment, and asks you to produce designs for two different interpretations of the fairies:

- as vicious, spiteful, selfish creatures, full of wild emotions and with quick tempers, at odds with the natural world they live in
- as changeable but more humanlike, in tune with their natural environment, able to appear and disappear at will.

Work in your group to produce designs, or descriptions if you don't like drawing, to fit both these interpretations. To help you, consider all that you already know about the behaviour of the fairies.

In your designs, include information about and sketches of:

- fabrics for costumes: colours, textures
- the style of costume, including cloaks
- any jewellery
- head-dresses (for example, made of flowers), crown?
- hair, wigs (for example, covered with berries)
- make-up
- any props, for example flowers, sword
- footwear.

## Lost in the wood                          *lines 41–71*

Hermia and Lysander are worn out with walking through the
wood. Lysander has forgotten the way!

With a partner, look at Hermia's reasons for asking him to lie
further away from her, as they lie down to sleep. Pick out all
her key words, and note them down.

## Enter Puck                               *lines 72–89*

First read Puck's lines, in pairs, emphasizing the rhythm of this
different verse form. You'll notice how this rhythm makes the
rhyme more noticeable, too.

Then discuss:

■   what Puck thinks he is doing in lines 72–89
■   what he is actually doing.

Pick out words and phrases which reveal Puck's attitude to
Hermia and Lysander (whom he thinks is Demetrius!).

## Helena                                   *lines 90–140*

Suddenly, Helena is loved – but by the wrong man. Puck put
the juice in Lysander's not Demetrius' eyes.

In groups of four, discuss the feelings Helena expresses in lines
94–105

■   towards Hermia
■   about her own physical appearance
■   concerning Demetrius' rejection of her.

Pick out two lines which sum up what she's saying. Then two
of you read Helena's words, two of you read Lysander's words,
reading pairs of lines so that you read (and hear) the rhyming
couplets. Try different ways of reading their words (tones of
voice, expression, speed) to emphasize Helena's reaction to
Lysander's absolute love for her.

Discuss how you feel Helena copes (lines 114–116) with
Lysander's unexpected declaration of love. Note down your
thoughts about these two characters at this point in the play.

### Helena reacts                                    *lines 129–140*

In pairs, discuss
- why you think Helena asks so many questions in lines 129–134
- why she repeats words, for example in line 131
- what she thinks Lysander is up to.

### Lysander's new love                              *lines 141–150*

The love potion certainly works. Look at what Lysander is saying now about Hermia. Pick out all the words which show his loathing of her. Note them down.

### Hermia abandoned                                 *lines 151–162*

As a class, stand in a circle to read Hermia's lines, taking it in turns to read up to a punctuation mark. Try reading these lines in different ways, for example, quietly and sadly, hysterically, shouting. Which way works best?

### 'What a dream was here!'

In this scene, the power of dreams and illusions is shown, arising from sleep and magic flower juice.

Look back over the act and complete this simple grid to keep track of who slept, who dreamt, who was under the influence of magic or illusion, who talked about or worked magic or illusions.

| Slept | Dreamt | Under influence of magic/ illusion | Talked about/ worked magic/ illusion |
|-------|--------|-----------------------------------|--------------------------------------|
| Titania Lysander Hermia | Hermia – about a serpent | Lysander | Oberon – invisible<br><br>Puck – went round the earth in 40 minutes |

## On reflection

On your own, produce one of the following pieces of writing:
- Helena's diary entry, which will include her feelings about Demetrius' treatment of her, and her suspicions about Lysander's real intentions
- a letter from Lysander to Hermia explaining why he no longer loves her, but loves her best friend instead
- a love letter from Lysander to Helena.

## Act 2: in and out of love

Draw a diagram to show whom each of the following characters loves at the end of Act 2: Lysander, Helena, Hermia, Demetrius. Compare this with the diagram you drew at the end of Act 1.

## What is going on?

In groups of four, work out freeze frames to show the state of relationships in the play up to here:
- Demetrius and Helena
- Lysander and Helena
- Helena and Hermia
- Hermia and Lysander
- Titania and Oberon
- Puck and everybody else.

Choose one of your freeze frames to show to the class.

Remember that Titania is still asleep on stage.

# Act 3 scene 1

*The same night. The wood.*
*(Titania is asleep on stage.)*
*The Mechanicals' unintentionally comical rehearsal of 'Pyramus and Thisbe' is interrupted by the magical intervention of Puck, the practical joker. This is the first scene in the play in which a fairy (Titania) and a human character (Bottom) speak to each*

*other. The scene separates Bottom from his fellow Mechanicals (who flee back to Athens) leaving him on his own.*

### Play within a play                        *lines 1–102*

The Mechanicals meet to rehearse, and discover even more problems. Look back at the work you did for Act 1 scene 2 (page 27), and carry on with the same character which you had then as you work in your groups. Read through the scene in parts, and look for clues to increase your understanding of your character from what he says in the scene.

Then add to your earlier list (from Act 1 scene 2) the new problems that come up in the rehearsal.

Discuss in your group the nature of these problems. Are they really serious? What do they tell you about the Mechanicals' idea of the audience they will be acting to? Note down your opinions.

### Puck's pranks                              *lines 103–108*

As a class, divide into three groups.
Group 1 prepares a reading of Puck's lines.
Group 2 creates mimes for each place or animal which Puck mentions.
Group 3 adds appropriate sound effects for each line.
The three groups now combine to present these lines.

Puck destroys the rehearsal, and turns Bottom into an ass. He has already turned Lysander's love away from Hermia to Helena, and soon Titania will fall in love with Bottom the ass.

Look back at Puck in the play and remind yourself of what he likes doing. What gives him the most pleasure?

### Bottom makes an ass of himself!

In pairs, read Titania and Bottom's conversation (lines 126–195). Either take it in turns to read lines, or play a character each.

Pick out the compliments Titania pays to Bottom which show that she is under a magic spell, and say them to a partner in the kind of voice you think she would use.

 In the last scene in which you met Titania talking to a man, she was with Oberon (Act 2 scene 1 lines 60–145). Read these lines again. With a partner, make up two freeze frames between you to show how Titania behaves differently on each occasion. Show them to another pair and compare your different approaches.

### Beauty and the beast

With your partner, look closely at the two photographs of Titania and Bottom on page 43. Talk about the impression you gain of Titania in each photograph.

Make a note of:

■ which presentation of Titania you prefer and why
■ how you react to Bottom's unruffled treatment of the fairies. What does this show you about him?
■ how you react to Titania's parting line: 'Tie up my love's tongue, bring him silently'. What do you think she is thinking when she says this?

## Act 3 scene 2

*Later the same night. Another part of the wood.*
*The effects of the magic flower juice, mistakenly applied to the wrong mortal's eyes, are revealed in this chaotic, quarrelsome scene. Various types of love are explored. The act closes by opening up the possibility of the magic mistakes being sorted out – the business of Act 4.*

This very long scene (464 lines) cannot be broken down into shorter parts because the stage is never empty. When you have finished working on it, you might like to produce a chart to show who is on stage when.

### Puck                                            *lines 6–34*

Puck tells Oberon about events the audience has already seen. Look at his lines, and discuss with your partner what effect this has on the audience. Why does the audience need to be told the same thing twice?

 ### Put Puck in the hot seat

Question Puck about his actions so far in the play. One of you be Puck, and answer questions asked by the class. The class should try to find out what Puck's attitudes are towards other characters, and make Puck realize the harm he has done.

Now, as Puck, write a short, boastful speech in modern English to a fairy in which you

- explain what has happened to Titania
- offer your opinion of the Mechanicals
- describe your own key role in what has happened.

Include words or phrases from the text if possible, e.g. 'thick-skin' to describe one of the Mechanicals. Make your feelings about what has happened very clear: are you excited, proud, guilty . . .?

### Demetrius and Hermia argue                    *lines 43–81*

Pick out lines which illustrate these points in the argument between Demetrius and Hermia, and write them down:

- she thinks Demetrius has killed Lysander
- she cannot believe Lysander would leave her
- she calls Demetrius a coward
- he loves her
- he hates Lysander
- he has not killed Lysander.

How would you describe the mood of Hermia and Demetrius in these lines?

### Puck and Oberon                                *lines 88–121*

Puck and Oberon have very different views of the humans.

After you have read the lines with your partner, pick out the key lines spoken by each of them which sum up their attitudes. Write them down.

They remain on stage, watching what goes on after Oberon has squeezed juice into Demetrius' eyes.

### Helena                                        *lines 122–176*

Ever since Lysander had the love juice put on his eyes, he has been pursuing Helena.

In pairs, improvise the conversation which Helena and Lysander could have had off stage which ends with him saying to her, 'Why should you think that I should woo in scorn?'

Helena is at her wits' end: how can she convince Lysander that she doesn't believe him? Things are made even worse when Demetrius wakes up and starts saying the same things to her.

Work in threes to produce a shortened version of this part of the scene, giving each character no more than ten or so of their original lines.

Present your version to the class, making the feelings of each character obvious by the way you speak their lines. Compare versions.

### The joys of friendship past            *lines 192–219*

When Hermia comes in, Helena can't help thinking her friend is part of the same game, and appeals to Hermia's past friendship for her.

In your group of four, re-read Helena's description of her friendship with Hermia. Take it in turns to read a line. Produce a list of the descriptions she gives of the closeness of their friendship. Illustrate one of them each and add the appropriate line(s) of text, for example:

'Is all the counsel that we two have shar'd –
The sisters' vows, the hours that we have spent...'

## Four lovers argue

*lines 220–344*

In fours, work on this long part of the scene, reading and performing it in parts, and then as a class look at the work of some of the groups.

Use these ideas to help you, and to make the lines come alive:

- whenever you talk about someone, point at them
- whenever you talk to someone, go right up to them
- work out the actions you should do from the lines (there are few stage directions in Shakespeare!). For example, at line 260 when Lysander says, 'Hang off, thou cat, thou burr', Hermia must be holding tightly on to him
- remember this is an argument, a furious row, and the characters shout, get angry, insult each other, get upset.

 ## The insults game

Use the words spoken by the characters to find out what it feels like to be insulted.

Divide the class into two lines, which stand facing each other at either end of the room. Each of you has an opposite number, who is your target. When you shout your insult, aim it at your target person. Split the list of insults below between the two lines of people. Each line takes it in turns to shout, all together, one of its insults at the opposite line of targets. Every time your line shouts an insult, you take one small step towards the opposite line. Look and sound really aggressive. Stop before you reach the opposite line!

Insulting words from the scene for you to shout:

> you are unkind
> the hate I bare thee made me leave thee so
> injurious Hermia
> most ungrateful maid
> away, you Ethiope
> hang off, thou cat, thou burr
> vile thing, let loose
> or I will shake thee from me like a serpent
> why are you grown so rude?
> out, tawny Tartar, out
> out, loathed medicine

> hated potion, hence
> I do hate thee
> you juggler
> you canker-blossom
> you thief of love
> you counterfeit
> you puppet you
> thou painted maypole
> vixen
> little
> you dwarf
> you minimus, of hindering knot-grass made
> you bead, you acorn

When you have finished, write down in your journal how you felt as you shouted insults and they were shouted at you. Make a note of any which stick in your mind.

## You Ethiope, tawny Tartar – the language of abuse

In fours, look carefully at the language which the lovers use to insult each other. How do they try to hurt each other?

Throughout the play, Hermia is consistently referred to as very small, and dark-skinned. Do you think the words 'Ethiope' and 'Tartar' are used in a racist way here? If you were Hermia, how would you feel about it?

How would you convince an actor playing the part of Lysander to go ahead and say these words (lines 257 and 263) if he said he found them offensive?

Write down your answers to all these questions.

## Oberon is angry                                      *lines 345–395*

Yet again, Puck has made a mess of things.

Look at the lines with your partner and then write down:
■ Oberon's orders to Puck
■ Oberon's own intentions towards Titania.

Note down what Puck and Oberon say about 'damned spirits' and themselves.

## 'Overcast the night . . . with drooping fog'

As a class, mime walking around the room as if you are in a thick fog, at night, with overhanging trees, and on very rough ground. Try it:

- walking as slowly and carefully as you can
- running as fast as you can, peering to look for someone
- closing your eyes and feeling your way with your hands.

### Fog on stage

Discuss possible ways of creating fog or mist on stage. In your journal, mention the advantages and disadvantages of leaving the fog to the audience's imagination: that is, no mist is visible but is created in the audience's minds by the actions and words of Demetrius and Lysander as they grope their way across the stage.

### Night and day                                   *lines 379–393*

Read again Puck's description of night (lines 379–387) and Oberon's references to morning (lines 389–393). Did you notice that night and morning are personified – that is, presented as if they were people?

Discuss with a partner the descriptions of night, day, and the supernatural which you have just read.

Choose a word, line, or phrase from either speech and use it as a stimulus for a piece of descriptive writing, for example 'swift dragons'. Your writing can be in verse or prose, and illustrated if you wish. Let your imagination take over.

### Puck plays the mimic                            *lines 401–430*

What is the result on stage of Puck's being able to mimic Lysander and Demetrius' voices so convincingly? In groups of three, read the lines. The person reading Puck's lines should try to mimic the voices of the other two – not an easy task!

### Stage plan

Read on to the end of the act. Pay particular attention to the entrances, exits, and stage directions relating to sleep.

Using a copy of the stage plan on page 94, mark on the paper where each of the four lovers is lying at the end of Act 3.

## Sleep: the four young lovers

Discuss:
- the state of mind in which each of the four lovers falls asleep
- what each hopes or plans will happen when they awake.

 ## Puck's magic                                                    *lines 448–464*

As a class, stand in a circle. One of you lies in the middle of the circle as a tired, sleeping Lysander. In your class circle, read Puck's lines 448–464, reading a word each. Then distribute the lines round the group to pairs of readers. While Lysander remains sleeping in the middle of your circle, each pair walks over to Lysander, reads their line, mimes squeezing the juice and returns to the circle. Do this until all of Puck's lines have been read.

Experiment with ways of using your voices to convey a sense that these are *magical* powers Puck possesses.

## Dreams and illusions, night and time

Look back over Act 3, working with a partner.

*Either* collect up all the references to dreams, sleep, eyes, and illusions, and write them up on a large sheet of paper with the names of the appropriate characters.

*Or* collect up all the references to night, light, time, moon, spirits, and do the same as above.

Display your work, and compare what you have found with other groups. Discuss what impressions these words give you about the events that have already happened.

## Act 3: in and out of love

Draw a diagram to show whom each of the following characters loves at the end of Act 3: Lysander, Helena, Hermia, Demetrius, Titania. Compare this with the diagrams you drew at the ends of Acts 1 and 2.

# Act 4 scene 1

*Nearly morning. The wood.*
*In this busy scene, characters under the influence of the magic*
*flower juice, who were in love with the wrong person, are now*
*released from the spell: Lysander loves Hermia again; Titania*
*loves Oberon. Harmony is restored.*

## Making a scene diagram                    *lines 1–219*

This scene is complex because so many characters – human and
fairy – enter, exit, wake, or sleep. The first section of the scene
features Bottom, Titania, and four fairies. What are the other
sections? How would you divide up the scene? If you divide the
scene at every point where characters enter, exit, wake, or speak,
it falls into seven separate sections. Either copy out the grid
below and complete it, or devise your own way of writing down
the sections in the scene. For each section of the scene, select
two or three key lines to sum up what happens.

| Section | Characters speaking | Line numbers when they speak | Line when characters enter, exit, sleep or wake | Key lines to sum up the action |
|---|---|---|---|---|
| 1 | Bottom, Titania and four fairies | 1–45 | 41 – fairies exit<br><br>45 – Titania and Bottom sleep | |
| 2 | Oberon and Puck | 46–75 | 46 – Puck enters<br><br>Oberon comes forward | |

### Bottom and Titania                                   *lines 1–45*

As he often does, Oberon watches. His wife Titania showers love and attention on Bottom. Does Oberon enjoy what he sees?

Work in groups of six. Read or act out the lines, in parts, exaggerating the behaviour of all the characters: for example, Titania can be very loving, Bottom very like an ass, the fairies very small and anxious to please.

Write down everything Bottom says which shows him to be a 'human ass'.

### Oberon                                              *lines 46–75*

Work in pairs. Look closely at lines 46–75.

You are both Oberon.

One of you explains how you feel towards Bottom – on whom your wife dotes.

The other explains how you felt
- when you first learned whom Titania had fallen in love with (Act 3 scene 2 lines 6–35)
- how you now feel about it
- how you managed to get Titania to give you the Indian boy
- how you intend to release her from your spell.

Now work in groups of four. Split into two pairs.

One pair prepares and presents a case arguing that Oberon is justified in his behaviour towards Titania in the play so far.

The other pair prepares and presents a case arguing that Oberon is not justified in his behaviour towards Titania in the play so far.

Both pairs should use quotations from the play to support their arguments.

When you have finished, decide which pair had the easier task – and why.

Finally, on your own, write up, using quotations, the conflicting interpretations of Oberon's character and his treatment of his wife.

## Sleeping and waking

During this scene six characters sleep at one time or another.

Look carefully through the scene to find the stage directions for characters to sleep and wake. Copy out the chart below and use your knowledge to complete it. You will need to look back to Act 3 for some of the information which you need.

|  | Titania | Bottom | Helena | Hermia | Lysander | Demetrius |
|---|---|---|---|---|---|---|
| Lines sleeping | 46–75 | | | | | |
| Reason for sleeping | Tired – allows Oberon to apply magic herb | | | | | |
| Line wakes | 76 | | | | | |
| Cue or reason for waking | Oberon wakes her | | | | | |
| What is difference when character wakes | No longer in love with Bottom. Reunited with Oberon. Has given Indian boy to Oberon. | | | | | |

### 'What visions have I seen'                    *line 76*

Titania is the second person to tell of a dream she has had. Who was the first?

Write a detailed diary entry for Titania at this point. Include her impressions of:

■ her first meeting with Bottom (Act 3 scene 1): her reactions to his singing, his looks, falling in love with him, her fairies tending him
■ her next memory of him as he jokes with her attendants (Act 4 scene 1) and her feelings towards him
■ awaking as if from a dream to see Oberon and the ass with whom she thought she had been in love
■ her desire to get Oberon to explain how she had come to be sleeping near to four mortals.

### Puck, Oberon, and Titania              *lines 93–102*

These spirits must now take care: Puck hears the morning lark, which tells them all they must fly off, following the night round the earth.

Read their lines in threes, taking parts. Make each rhyming word sound long and drawn-out, and experiment with making your voices sound as though they are fading away.

### Theseus and Hippolyta                  *lines 103–127*

Read lines 103–127.

Discuss how Theseus tries to impress and please Hippolyta and how she reacts.

Look back to Theseus and Hippolyta's only other conversation (Act 1 scene 1 lines 1–19). Do you think that their relationship has developed? Consider:

■ how they speak to each other in both of these conversations
■ what they talk about
■ how many times Hippolyta speaks in both conversations.

Are you convinced that they love each other?

## Egeus                                    *lines 128–131*

Use these lines as the basis for Egeus' diary entry for the day, in
which he also thinks back to the time two days before when
Hermia defied him. Make the answers to these questions part of
his diary entry:

- Did he know that she has run away from home?
- Does he sound surprised to find her here in the wood?

## Young lovers                            *lines 141–186*

In lines 141–186, the fortunes of the four young lovers change.
In groups of four, read their lines and discuss their behaviour
and words now that they are back to 'normal'.

## 'Egeus, I will overbear your will'

In your journal, write down what you think in response to the
following questions:

1   How do you react to Theseus' decision, bearing in mind
    what he said in Act 1 scene 1 lines 119–126?
2   Why do you think he has changed his mind?
    Use the lines which Demetrius (lines 160–176) and
    Lysander (lines 151–153) have just spoken to help you.
3   Why do you think that Lysander and Demetrius speak,
    whilst Hermia and Helena remain silent?

## Hermia's plight                         *lines 139–185*

Remind yourself of:

- the choices which Theseus gave to Hermia (Act 1 scene 1
  lines 86–90)
- what Hermia had planned to do in the face of these choices.

Consider – she has just been caught, eloping, by her father and
the Duke. Write Hermia's thoughts and feelings from when she
wakes up (line 139) to when Theseus changes the course of her
life (up to line 185). Which lines spoken by Lysander,
Demetrius, or her father would she react to in particular?

### Headline news

Write the front page newspaper report which covers the news of the four missing lovers, found together in the wood – under mysterious circumstances. Think about who discovered them, and when; how Egeus was overruled; the way Theseus ignored Egeus' appeal to the law of Athens; and the three forthcoming weddings.

### Oberon's prediction

During Act 4, Oberon has already predicted that all of the lovers will marry the next day. Find, read aloud, and write down the two lines in which he makes this prediction.

### Puzzled lovers                                        *lines 187–199*

In groups of four, read the lovers' lines in a dreamy, puzzled way. Pick out words and phrases which suggest their confusion and uncertainty and whisper them to each other. The lovers are the third set of characters to wake up from dreams.

### Bottom wakes                                          *lines 200–219*

Read Bottom's lines as he wakes up (lines 200–219). Discuss with a partner

■ what he thinks he is doing on awaking
■ how we know that he is confused (Which words does he repeat? Which phrases are contradictory?)

Bottom's is the fourth awakening from a dream. He is obviously so startled by what he thinks he dreamt, that he never says what it was.

In pairs, prepare a TV chat show in which Bottom is interviewed about his experiences in the wood, by writing out the interviewer's questions and Bottom's replies. Use what Bottom says here, and what he said earlier during the rehearsal, as the basis for your interview. Rehearse and then present your interview to the class.

# Act 4 scene 2

*Morning of the next day. Athens: a room in Quince's house.
In this very short scene, the Mechanicals are reunited with
Bottom and learn that their production of 'Pyramus and Thisbe'
has been put on the list of possible entertainments for the Duke.
As the play nears its end, we return to the city where it all began
– Athens.*

## Bottom lost and found

In groups of six, read this scene. Indicate by changing your
expression of voice and face, how you react when Bottom enters.

## 'He cannot be heard of'                         *line 2*

The Mechanicals think that Bottom has been carried away
('transported') by spirits. Write the MISSING poster which they
might have produced for Bottom.

Include as much factual information as you can:
■  his job
■  where and when he was last seen
■  what he was wearing on his head at the time
■  why he is needed so urgently
■  who is looking for him
■  how long he has been missing
■  who is suspected of taking him
■  his personality.

Add an artist's impression of Bottom as he looked when he
disappeared.

## The weddings

We only have Snug's report that the three couples are now
married. In pairs, discuss why you think the weddings take place
off-stage.

Write two newspaper reports of the weddings: one in the style of
a tabloid newspaper which includes an interview with the furious

Egeus, and the other in the style of a broadsheet. Include interviews with some of the characters who have just married, and one or two details about their past lives. Think carefully of the wording for your headlines.

## Act 5 scene 1

*After supper, on the evening of the next day. Athens: the palace of Theseus.*
*The wedding night celebrations form one final scene which brings together the different groups of human characters – nobles and Mechanicals – and the human and fairy worlds.*

### Reactions                                      *lines 1–27*

The scene opens with Theseus and Hippolyta discussing the lovers' reports of what had happened the previous night in the wood.

As a class, read Theseus and Hippolyta's lines by punctuation marks.

Make a note in your journal of what you learn about Theseus' and Hippolyta's characters from their differing reactions to the lovers' tales.

### 'The lunatic, the lover, and the poet'      *lines 2–22*

Theseus describes the different qualities of the lunatic, the lover, and the poet – what is unique about the thoughts and behaviour of each, but also what they have in common. Draw a Venn diagram like the one opposite to sum this up.

Then spot as many words as you can in Theseus' speech which are about imagination. Note them down. What is there about this play that makes these words appropriate? Is Theseus the best character to say them? Note down your answers.

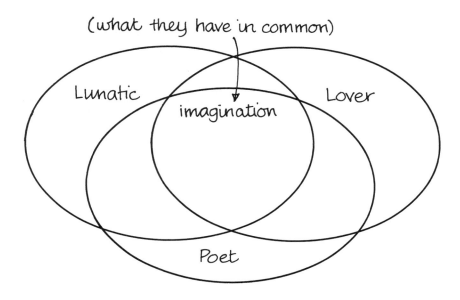

(what they have in common)

Lunatic

imagination

Lover

Poet

**'What revels are in hand?'**                              *line 36*

Why do you think that Philostrate does not read out the list of possible entertainments, but hands it to Theseus to read aloud?

In groups of four, read the list of entertainments, each reading out a description of an entertainment. They start on lines 44, 48, 52, and 56.

Pick out and read aloud the contradictions in lines 56–60. What impressions do they give you about the Mechanicals' play?

**'It is nothing . . .'**                              *lines 61–81*

Read Philostrate's impression of the Mechanicals' play, based on a rehearsal which he has watched. Look back to the Mechanicals' first discussion (Act 1 scene 2), and their rehearsal which you have read (Act 3 scene 1). Discuss, then make a note of whether you agree with:

■ Philostrate's comment on the play
■ his impression of the Mechanicals (lines 72–74).

How does he try to persuade Theseus not to choose this play?

### Theseus rules                                    *lines 82–105*

In pairs, read Theseus' decision to watch the play:

> ' . . . we will hear it' (line 76)
> 'I will hear that play.' (line 81)

Try out different ways of reading the lines, for example angrily, commandingly, calmly. Discuss together how you could read the second line differently from the first.

How does Theseus speak differently to Philostrate and to Hippolyta about the play?

### 'Our sport shall be to take what they mistake'
                                              *lines 85–105*

Read Theseus and Hippolyta's difference of opinion over whether to watch this play. Discuss, then write down:

- Hippolyta's objections and what this shows about her
- Theseus' answers to her objections
- why you think he refers to speeches which 'great clerks' have prepared for him in the past. What point is he trying to make?
- whether you think Theseus' motives for choosing this play are honourable. Does he choose this play so that he can laugh at the Mechanicals' attempts, or as a way of thanking them for their efforts?

 ### Pyramus and Thisbe: the performance   *lines 108–335*

Remind yourself of the story of 'Pyramus and Thisbe' (*Ways In* page 17).

As a class, cast the following parts: Theseus, Hippolyta, Hermia, Helena, Lysander, Demetrius, Philostrate, Quince, Bottom, Flute, Snout, Snug, Starveling, courtiers who watch, move and whisper to each other, servants who attend on the nobles, bringing in food and drink. Have one person as director. Everyone in the class should have a part to play. The director should organize the distribution of parts, make sure that characters come in at the right time, direct where they should stand and move, and check that their lines can be heard by everyone.

On your feet, read the play straight through: stop at line 335.

In your journal, note:
- what went well in your read-through
- how it could have been improved.

### 'This fellow doth not stand upon points' *lines 108–125*

In pairs, read Quince's prologue (lines 108–117) by punctuation marks. Because Quince puts his punctuation in the wrong places, he says the opposite of what he means.

Re-write Quince's prologue, putting the punctuation in the correct places, and read it aloud with your partner. Discuss:
- why you think Quince mispunctuates his prologue
- how you would advise an actor to deliver the prologue: nervously? Quickly? Excitedly? Hesitantly?

Read Theseus', Hippolyta's and Lysander's reactions to the prologue. Give your opinions of the three similes (lines 118–125) which they use to describe Quince's performance. Do they accurately sum up how Quince spoke?

### Pyramus and Thisbe: the dumbshow *lines 126–150*

While Quince describes the play for the audience before they see it, the Mechanicals present it as dumbshow. As Quince reads lines 126–150, Pyramus (Bottom), Thisbe (Flute), Wall (Snout), Moonshine (Starveling), and Lion (Snug) present the action he describes in dumbshow, making clear what the play will be about.

How do Theseus and Demetrius react to Quince's words?

### Wall

How to present a wall on stage posed a considerable technical problem for the Mechanicals. Look back to remind yourself of their earlier discussion of this technical problem (Act 3 scene 1 lines 58–68).

Look at how Wall was presented differently on stage in two productions.

Discuss the importance of Wall in the play of 'Pyramus and Thisbe'. Does it matter *how* he is presented?

## Asides

Throughout the performance of 'Pyramus and Thisbe', members of the audience of nobles pass comment. In small groups, pick out, read aloud and chart these asides.

Now discuss:

■ which character most often begins and ends the asides
■ which character speaks least often in the asides
■ which characters say nothing in the asides. Mime what you think the silent observers were doing. Why do you think they do not get involved in the asides?

How do you react to the asides? Why do you think the characters made them? Are they funny? What do you feel about the characters making them? Write down your opinions.

## Actors and audience converse!          *lines 180–185*

In pairs, read Theseus' aside (lines 180–181) and Bottom's reply to it (lines 182–185). What does this reply, in the middle of a performance, tell you about Bottom's view of acting? How do you think he would say these words? Try out different ways of saying them and different facial expressions which Theseus could have shown.

Do you think that the Mechanicals were intended to hear the nobles' asides? Experiment by saying one of the asides in two different ways:

■ as if it were meant to be overheard
■ as if it were intended to be part of a private conversation.

## Snug (as Lion)          *lines 215–222*

Look back in the play to where the Mechanicals talked about their problems when presenting a lion to an audience including 'ladies' (Act 1 scene 2 lines 66–78, Act 3 scene 1 lines 26–45). In small groups, read out these lines.

Now with these concerns in mind read Lion's actual performance (Act 5 scene 1 lines 215–222). How well did Snug, as the Lion, cope with their anticipated problems?

In your journal, write down how the audience of nobles reacted to Snug's thoughtful explanation that he is not a lion but a joiner. Did they think that he was terrifying?

###  Bottom (as Pyramus) dies – eventually! *lines 285–296*

As a class, read Bottom's dying speech as Pyramus: take it in turns for pairs to read a line. When the line 'Thus die I, thus, thus, thus!' is read, all act out Pyramus' death, stabbing yourself each time the word 'thus' is spoken. Read this final line together as a class, and all act out his tragic death. How would he die?

Discuss the effect which this prolonged death would have on the audience. Why do you think Bottom takes so long over his death scene?

###  Flute (as Thisbe)

Pick one of the class to play Bottom (as the dead Pyramus). The rest of the class stands in a circle around the 'corpse' and reads Flute's final speech, each reading up to the next punctuation mark. The readers should direct their words and looks towards Bottom, making them as exaggerated and comical as possible. Remember that Flute was initially worried about having to play a woman's role: Quince advised him to 'speak as small as you will' (Act 1 scene 2 lines 45–6). Bear this advice in mind as you read! When line 333 is read, all mime stabbing yourself.

### Language of love!

Look carefully at Thisbe's description of Pyramus. Pick out which fruit, flowers, and vegetables are used in comparison with parts of his body. Make a note of
- whether you think these comparisons are flattering
- how you think the audience would respond to them.

### 'Pyramus and Thisbe' – the verdict

Imagine that the Mechanicals' performance is reviewed by the media. As a class, split into groups and choose one of the following tasks:

*Either* write a performance review of the Mechanicals' production of 'Pyramus and Thisbe' for a tabloid newspaper.

*Or* write a performance review of the same performance for a 'quality' newspaper.

Before you work on these tasks, look at real tabloid and 'quality' papers to identify how their reports would differ in style, layout, and type of language used.

As a whole class, discuss each group's finished contribution.

Discuss what connection the theme of 'Pyramus and Thisbe' has with *A Midsummer Night's Dream*. Do you think it was an appropriate choice of entertainment for a wedding party?

## The wedding night

Theseus concludes the evening by pointing out the time: it is now midnight, 'almost fairy time'. So even in Athens itself, the fairies are part of the lives of humans.

As the humans leave the stage, to go to bed and to sleep, the new night, like the night before, belongs to the fairies. But they are now in Theseus' palace, and their intentions and actions are very different from what they were in the wood, outside Athens, on Midsummer Night.

When he is inside, Puck is a household fairy:

> In sixteenth-century England, Robin Goodfellow (Puck) was traditionally the spirit who kept the house clean and protected the household. 'Your grandam's maids were wont to set a bowl of milk before him . . . for grinding of malt or mustard, and sweeping the house at midnight.'
>
> Reginald Scot: *The Discoverie of Witchcraft* (1584)

Now he behaves quite differently, perhaps because the couples are *married*, and the palace has become 'a hallow'd house'.

Titania and Oberon are spirits who bless newly-married couples.

 Rehearse a performance of lines 357–410 as a whole class. Divide the class into pairs and a freeze frame group for Puck's lines

(357–377), have two people for Oberon and Titania (lines 378–387), and then work as a whole class for the rest of Titania's lines. The activities below give you more information about how to organize this.

 ### Puck
lines 357–377

Puck's words describe night, as the Elizabethans would have experienced it: dark, filled with the noises of wild animals and birds, and haunted by spirits of the dead. Puck and his kind run from the sun, 'following darkness like a dream'.

Rehearse a reading of these lines, each pair speaking one line. Bring out the contrast between the 'night' lines (357–370) and the more playful 'fairy' lines (371–377). The freeze frame group prepares freeze frames to show lines 357–358, lines 364–365, and lines 368–369. Move into your freeze frames as the lines are read.

 ### Oberon and Titania
lines 378–387

Two readers practise these lines. Work out a way to show, through your voices and the way you look at each other, that Titania and Oberon are now united and at peace.

 ### Titania's lines
lines 388–410

Allocate one line to each person in the class. If there are not enough lines, give some lines to pairs. Learn your own line, so you don't need the script. Stand in a circle and say your lines in turn, then hold hands round the circle and move in time to the words, taking four steps on each line. You can vary these movements – to the right or left. For some of the lines, you can move into the centre of your circle as you speak. Experiment till you feel you have a performance of the lines which conveys the sense of blessing, good wishes, and peace which the fairies bring to the married couples.

How does this magical blessing differ from the magical effects which Oberon and Titania had on the mortal world in Act 2 scene 1 lines 88–117?

Write a modern blessing to be read in the house of a newly-married couple. Include mention of children the couple may produce.

 ## Puck

*lines 411–426*

Two readers split these lines between them. The rest of the class stands round them in a circle.

If you are one of the readers of Puck's lines, go up to anyone in the circle to say your line, then move across to someone else for your next line.

Meanwhile, the class claps in rhythm to the lines – four beats to each line – starting very, very quietly and very strictly in rhythm, and gradually building up to a climax on the line, 'Give me your hands, if we be friends', when your rhythmic clapping should become proper applause!

This will need some rehearsal.

Then put the whole performance together from the beginning, moving quickly and silently into place for each new section.

## Last thoughts

Why do you think the play ends with fairy rather than mortal characters?

## 'You have but slumber'd here'

How do you react to Puck's statement that while you have been watching the play you have been sleeping – that it was 'but a dream'? Make a note in your journal of your reaction to this unusual idea.

# Overview

### Character profiles

These character profiles can be used for revision or for introducing characters before the play is read. See pages 73–74 for details of activities based on them.

### *Theseus*

You are the Duke of Athens. You have defeated the armies of the Amazons. Although you wooed her with violence, you are eagerly looking forward to marrying the Amazons' warrior Queen, Hippolyta, in four days' time. Love plays an important part in your life at this time. You at first support Egeus, one of your nobles, in applying the full strength of the law to Egeus' daughter, Hermia, who refuses the marry the man chosen by her father. Later you override Egeus by disregarding the law, and encouraging Hermia to marry the man she has chosen. You are fond of hunting and other entertainments to while away the time – you spend much of your time in this play waiting. You marry Hippolyta in a joint wedding ceremony with the two young couples whom you have helped. You select an unlikely entertainment, prepared by a group of workmen, to be performed at the celebrations on your wedding night.

### *Egeus*

You are an Athenian nobleman. You are furious when your daughter refuses to co-operate with your marriage plans for her. You believe that you have absolute rights and control over your daughter's life. You are a proud man, stubborn and absolutely determined to get your own way. You are willing to sacrifice your own daughter's happiness – and, if necessary, her life – rather than be disobeyed. With Theseus and his party, you are shocked to discover your daughter in the woods – eloping! You are disappointed when your wishes are overruled by Duke Theseus who gives your daughter permission to marry the man of her choice, Lysander.

### Hermia

You are the daughter of Egeus. You are in love with Lysander but your father objects to him and insists that you must marry Demetrius. You are sure that your father is not the best judge of your future husband and boldly say so – even though you risk his wrath. The Duke gives you three impossible choices if you continue to defy your father. Rather than submit, you agree to elope with Lysander, travelling with him through the woods outside Athens to his aunt's house. You pity your best friend, Helena, who loves Demetrius – who loves you – although you have made it clear to both of them that you love Lysander. Your reputation and virginity are very important to you. Even when you are both lost in the wood, you make sure that Lysander sleeps a distance away from you. You are utterly bewildered when Lysander abruptly falls in love with your friend Helena and stops loving you. You can make no sense of the strange things that happen in the wood on Midsummer Night, and are only too glad that Lysander's love for you is restored. You marry him in a joint ceremony with two other couples.

### Helena

You are upset because the man who recently loved you now wants to marry your best friend, Hermia. You envy Hermia and wish that you looked more like her to win back the man you fervently love. You feel so desperate that you betray to Demetrius Hermia's secret plan to elope. You risk your own reputation by following Demetrius to the wood. You are very hurt when he spurns you and leaves you, unprotected, in the wood at night. When first Lysander, and then Demetrius himself, suddenly declare their passionate love for you, you can only think they are playing a cruel joke on you. You even think Hermia is part of a game to mock you. You are surprised but delighted when Demetrius finally loves you again and marries you.

### Lysander

You are in love with Egeus' daughter, Hermia. Her father objects to you as a husband, even though you feel your claim is as good as Demetrius'. You are so desperate to marry Hermia, and to save her from the fate threatened by Theseus, that you run away with her to the wood outside Athens. When you are lost in the wood at night you try to take advantage of her, but don't force her, and agree to sleep some distance from her. Without knowing why, you suddenly decide that you hate Hermia and love Helena. You completely abandon Hermia. When she finds you, you declare your love for Helena, in front of her. Your love for Helena is so strong that you and Demetrius, both rivals for her love, go off to fight each other. When you are woken up the next morning by the Duke's hunting party, you cannot understand what has been going on. You feel afraid of Egeus, but the Duke supports your love for Hermia, and allows you to marry her. You enjoy the play of 'Pyramus and Thisbe'.

### Demetrius

You were recently in love with Helena, but you now love her best friend, Hermia. You insist on marrying her, even though she tells you that she does not love you but loves Lysander. When Helena tells you of Hermia's plan to elope, you follow – and Helena follows you. You are exasperated with Helena as she chases you, swearing her love for you. You harshly tell Helena that you do not love her, and you leave her alone, unprotected, in the wood. You do not care about her or her well-being. Suddenly, without knowing why, you love Helena again and harshly reject Hermia. You are so infatuated that you rush off to fight your rival Lysander. You are pleased to be allowed to marry Helena in the end. You enjoy the play of 'Pyramus and Thisbe'.

### Oberon

You are the King of the Fairies, and are most powerful in the wood, which is your territory. You are having a furious argument with your wife Titania because she refuses to give up to you an Indian boy in her care. You feel that your wife should obey you, and you accuse her of being unfaithful. You do not care about the effects of your quarrel on the natural world and on humans, as long as you make her give way. You maliciously take revenge on your wife by using magic, and exploiting the unexpected presence of a human in the wood at night. Your revenge is to see her humiliated. Ironically, you feel concerned when you see a mortal man treat a woman harshly, and you try to help her. You try to help mortals and feel sorry when your well-meaning plans go wrong. You are angry with your servant, Puck, for making mistakes. Triumphantly, having got what you wanted from

Titania when she was under the spell of your magic, you are reconciled with her. With your fairy followers, you both bless the mortal couples on their wedding night.

### Titania

You are Queen of the Fairies. You accuse your husband Oberon of being unfaithful to you. You are proud and powerful and enjoy having your own way. You keep your promise, to an Indian priestess on her deathbed, that you will look after her son, and refuse to give the child up to your husband. You avoid your husband, but he intrudes on your fairy revels and disrupts them whenever possible. You are worried about the effects of this quarrel with Oberon on the mortal world. However, you cannot break your promise to the boy's mother and will not give your husband what he demands. After Oberon has used magic to make you fall in love with a mortal with an ass's head, you feel disgusted and amazed. While you were under the spell, you gave the boy up to Oberon. You and Oberon make peace and bless the wedding couples.

### Puck (Robin Goodfellow)

You are a mischievous fairy, servant to Oberon. You boast about the pranks which you enjoy playing on mortals, such as getting night travellers lost and pulling stools from under old women so that they fall on the floor. You can change shape and move very fast: you can travel around the earth in forty minutes. You enjoy obeying Oberon's commands and making him laugh. You take pleasure in helping him to take revenge on his wife, and in intervening in mortals' relationships. You do not have a very high opinion of mortals and are delighted when, through your mistake, their relationships go wrong. You have no conscience and do not worry if your practical jokes cause chaos in other people's lives. However, you will not risk Oberon's wrath and dutifully undo your mistakes. At the end you sweep the dust behind the door, an appropriate action for a household fairy like yourself.

### Bottom

You are an Athenian workman (a weaver). You are excited about the play which you and your friends are rehearsing for the Duke's wedding celebrations. You are confident, talkative, and enjoy acting and being the centre of attention! You offer to play all the parts in the play, feeling that you could act them better than anyone else. You worry that the noble ladies in your audience will not realize that you are all only acting and will be frightened by the lion's part. You have no idea what has happened to you in the wood where you have been rehearsing, and you cannot understand why all your friends run away when they see you with an ass's head. You very much enjoy the loving attention you receive from Titania and her attendants, but when the effects of the magic wear off, you can only remember that you had an amazing dream. What it was is beyond your power to tell. When your play is chosen for the entertainment at the wedding celebrations, you really come into your own, and give the best performance of Pyramus that you can.

## *Hippolyta*

You are the Queen of the Amazons, a race of women warriors who despised men and refused to marry. The only way Theseus could get you to marry him was by defeating you in battle. Like Theseus, you spend much of the time during the play waiting for your wedding day. You have little to say about Theseus' early arrangements for the wedding celebrations, but you seem to be disturbed by his treatment of Hermia in her dispute with her father Egeus. Theseus is eager for you to see and admire his pack of hounds on the morning of your wedding day. You remind Theseus that you have heard the best of hounds hunting in the past. You witness the discovery of the four young lovers in the woods – and Theseus overriding Athenian law to help them. You marry Theseus in a triple wedding ceremony alongside the young lovers. Unlike your husband, you are inclined to believe the four young lovers' strange tales about what happened to them in the wood. You try, unsuccessfully, to persuade Theseus not to choose the Mechanicals' play for your wedding celebrations as you fear that they will make fools of themselves.

The character profiles above represent the main characters. The following activities, based on the character profiles,

- can be done before work is started on the play, following the 'Who's Who?' activity on page 13
- can help you when you are revising characters after you have read the play.

## Profiles

Before you start to work on the play, divide the class into groups of six, and share the character profiles round each group. (It may help to make copies of them on separate sheets first.) Most of you will have two profiles each. Read and remember the information about your two characters, so that you can tell it from memory to your group.

Take the part of each of your characters in turn and tell your group about yourself from what you have read in the profile. Start off like this: 'My name is . . . and I am . . . ' Try not to look at your character profiles once your group has started the telling.

In your group, you may ask characters about themselves when they have finished talking. If you cannot answer a question, say 'I don't know yet', and make a note of the question.

## Quotations

When you have finished work on the play, work in the same groups of six that you were in for the 'profiles' activity, and fill out your characters' profiles by finding quotations from the play to illustrate six of the statements in the profiles.

Share your work with other groups, and compare the quotations you have chosen.

## Minor characters 1: bystanders

Quince, Snug, Starveling, Flute, Snout, Philostrate, Peaseblossom, Cobweb, Mustard Seed, Moth, and the fairy in Act 2 scene 1 are all minor characters.

Choose one of them and write about the events which they are involved in, or witness, from their point of view. Some examples would be:

■ Cobweb's description of Titania's infatuation with Bottom
■ Philostrate's reaction to Theseus' choice of the Mechanicals' play and his impression of the rehearsal of 'Pyramus and Thisbe'.

## Minor characters 2: the Mechanicals

Work in groups of six.

The Mechanicals never know what happened to Bottom, and why he suddenly appeared with an ass's head.

Imagine that the *Athens Observer* reporter who interviewed Quince in Act 1 scene 2 (see page 28) returns for a further extended interview with the company of actors. Work out the questions to ask the Mechanicals, and their answers. Write down the interview in playscript form, or prepare your questions and answers and then perform the interview for the class. For this performance, have one reporter asking the questions, and five Mechanicals (leave Bottom out of this).

The reporter is interested in:
■ the Mechanicals' fears for Bottom, and what happened to him
■ the play and the rehearsals
■ their preparations for the performance.

## Statement game 1

This game helps you go back over the play, and look at it again in detail, from different points of view.

Divide into seven groups. Each group:
■ takes one of the following statements
■ decides whether to agree or disagree with it, or whether to argue both sides of the case
■ finds evidence, including quotations, to support its argument
■ presents its case to the rest of the class
■ answers any objections or questions raised by the rest of the class.

1 Theseus was wrong to back down in Act 5 and allow Hermia and Lysander to marry, thus overriding Athenian law and breaking his own word.

2 Egeus was perfectly within his rights when he asked Theseus to use the law to make Hermia marry Demetrius – or face the death penalty.

3   Puck's tricks and magic never do anyone any harm, and his magic is more powerful than Oberon's.

4   Helena should have accepted offers of love from Lysander and Demetrius while she had the chance. After all, she had already been jilted once by Demetrius.

5   Oberon was justified in demanding the Indian boy from Titania, and in taking his revenge on her.

6   Lysander's treatment of Hermia was perfectly acceptable; after all, all is fair in love and war.

7   Theseus deliberately chose the play of 'Pyramus and Thisbe' so that he could laugh at the Mechanicals' pathetic attempt at acting.

## Women in the play

The world of *A Midsummer Night's Dream* is very much a man's world: even in the first scene, two women are shown to be dominated by men. You might find it interesting to discuss the way women are presented and treated in *A Midsummer Night's Dream* from a feminist point of view, and see if this opens up new ways of looking at the play.

Divide the class into six groups. Each group takes one of the situations listed below. Consider your group's chosen situation:
■   from a feminist point of view
■   from a conventional male point of view.

Present your opinions, from both sides, to the class, and answer any questions put by the class.

### Situations
■   Oberon's treatment of Titania
■   Demetrius' treatment of Helena
■   Egeus' treatment of Hermia
■   Theseus' treatment of Hippolyta
■   Theseus' treatment of Hermia
■   Lysander's treatment of Hermia.

## Puck and magic

You know quite a lot about Puck, and you have probably enjoyed and laughed at his tricks and mischief. Shakespeare seems to have put together old beliefs, superstitions, and folk customs to produce his character Puck.

If you think back over the action of the play, you will see that Puck causes all the confusion that takes place, sometimes as ordered by Oberon, sometimes by genuine mistake. He can behave as he does because he has certain magic powers, though he does not seem to be as powerful as Oberon. But although he does what Oberon asks him to do, he also acts quite independently of him. Whatever he does, he takes great delight in it and never shows any remorse.

Puck is also known as 'Robin Goodfellow'. Robin Goodfellow was a household goblin, and Shakespeare may have got some of his ideas for the character of Puck from popular superstitions and beliefs about Robin Goodfellow. For instance, people believed that he would help them with their domestic chores if he was well-treated, for example by being given a bowl of milk. In return, he would grind malt or mustard, and sweep the house at midnight.

But this could happen as well!

> He would chafe [get into a temper] exceedingly, if the maid or goodwife of the house, having compassion of his nakedness, laid any clothes for him. For in that case he sayeth, 'What have we here? Hempen, Hampen, here will I never more tread nor stampen.'
>
> Reginald Scot: *The Discoverie of Witchcraft* (1584)

It's quite surprising to find out that he went about with no clothes on! Shakespeare's Puck wears clothes, of course, and he doesn't lose his temper in the play, but he does sweep the house.

About two hundred years before Shakespeare, Chaucer's Wife of Bath complained about the way fairies were disappearing because churchmen and friars were going up and down the land blessing everything and saying prayers. She believed that this had killed off fairies, or at least frightened them away.

But, she says, this is what used to happen:

> In th'olde days of the King Arthur
> Of which that Britons speak great honour,
> All was this land fulfilled of fairies.
> The elf-queen, with her jolly company,
> Danced full oft in many a green mead.
>
> Chaucer: *The Canterbury Tales*

It would seem that by the time Shakespeare wrote *A Midsummer Night's Dream* in 1595, not everyone believed in fairies. Even so, Robin Goodfellow was still written about. In this extract from *The Ballad of Robin Goodfellow*, written in 1600, he boasts about how he entertains himself on Old Midsummer Day (our 5 July) by misleading people – just as he does in *A Midsummer Night's Dream*:

> Whene'er such wanderers I meet
> As from their night-sports they trudge home
> With counterfeiting voice I greet
> And call on them, with me to roam,
> Or else, unseen with them I go
> And frolic it, with Ho! Ho! Ho!

Look at the list of Puck's magic powers below, and find as many examples and quotations as you can from the play to complete the table:

| Magic powers | Examples | Quotations |
|---|---|---|
| Disrupts and changes the natural world | | |
| Takes on the shapes of other objects | | |
| Takes on the shapes of animals | | |
| Makes the sounds of animals | | |
| Spoils household jobs | | |
| Flies at great speed | | |
| Turns a human into an animal | | |
| Tricks people | | |

When you have completed your table, discuss with a partner what sort of magic this is. How powerful is it? What was it that Oberon could see, but Puck could not? Does this tell you anything about Puck's powers?

Now move on to look at the other supernatural beings in the play. What do they do? Do they show any magic powers or supernatural abilities? Consider the Fairy in Act 2 scene 1, Titania and her fairies Peaseblossom, Moth, Mustardseed, and Cobweb, and Oberon.

By the end of the play, which of these beings, including Puck, has proved to be the most powerful?

Note down your answers to these questions in your journal.

Look back at the photographs of Puck, taken from different productions of *A Midsummer Night's Dream*, on pages 77 and 80.

Do any of these Pucks fit in with your idea of him?

Do any of them fit in with what you've learned in this section?

Can you work out which moment of the play each photo is showing?

## Character and plot chart

The plot of *A Midsummer Night's Dream* is complex, as three separate but interconnecting strands weave through it. The strands are the worlds of the nobles, the fairies, and the Mechanicals. The following activity will help you to revise which characters and strands of the plot are presented in each scene.

| Act and scene | 1.1 | 1.2 | 2.1 | 2.2 | 3.1 | 3.2 | 4.1 | 4.2 | 5.1 |
|---|---|---|---|---|---|---|---|---|---|
| Theseus | * | | | | | | | | |
| Hippolyta | * | | | | | | | | |
| Egeus | * | | | | | | | | |
| Hermia | * | | | S* | | | | | |
| Helena | * | | | * | | | | | |
| Lysander | * | | | S*M | | | | | |
| Demetrius | * | | | * | | | | | |
| Oberon | | | | * | | | | | |
| Titania | | | | S*M | | | | | |
| Bottom | | | | | | | | | |
| Puck | | | | * | | | | | |
| Fairies | | | | * | | | | | |
| Mechanicals | | | | | | | | | |
| Philostrate | | | | | | | | | |
| Setting | Athens Theseus' Palace | | | wood | | | | | |

Using a grid like the one above,
- ■ mark with a * each scene in which a character speaks
- ■ print a letter 'S' if a character is on stage but is asleep for all or part of a scene
- ■ print a letter 'M' if a character is under the influence of magic for all or part of a scene.

The chart entries for Act 1 scene 1 and Act 2 scene 2 have been started for you.

You may wish to show which 'world' (Fairy, Nobility, or Mechanical) a character belongs to by using a different colour for the characters from each of the three different worlds.

In the final column, write the place in which each scene is set.

## Casting

In groups, work out how to cast this play using the smallest number of actors possible. No cutting of characters or scenes is allowed! Use the information from your character and plot chart to help you with this. One suggestion to start you off: some productions in the past have doubled up Theseus/Oberon and Hippolyta/Titania.

## Stream of consciousness

In this kind of writing, a character's inner thoughts and feelings are written down to convey as closely as possible the hesitations, inconsistencies, ramblings, and pauses you might find in someone's unspoken thoughts.

Imagine you are one of the characters who faces problems, uncertainties or self-doubt at any point in the play. Hermia and Helena are obvious examples, but Hippolyta might have a lot to think about in Act 1 scene 1, and Egeus, Oberon, and Titania all suffer from doubt, conflict or confusion.

Write a stream of consciousness piece, an inner monologue, for your chosen character, choosing two key moments from the play.

*Example: Oberon*

*Key moment/line:* Her dotage now I do begin to pity (Act 4 scene 1)
*Stream of consciousness:* I'm not sure I like seeing Titania behaving like this — my wife, with that half-human, half-ass — Puck was clever there — I never thought of that myself — but I'm sorry in a way — and yet I have got the boy from her —

# Plot

## Statement game 2

Divide into four groups. In your group:

- work on one of the following statements
- decide whether you agree, partially agree, or completely disagree with it
- find evidence, including brief quotations to support your viewpoint
- present your findings on a large sheet of paper, headed with your statement, on which you have written all your quotations, arguments, and ideas. When all the sheets of paper are finished, pin them up round the room, and have a look at each group's work.

### Statements

1  The influence of the fairy world on the world of mortals is always disastrous.

2  It is always the actions of the male characters which move the plot forward.

3  Magic is the only factor which causes events to occur in the play.

4  The events in Athens are the cause and consequence of the events in the wood.

## Bare bones

This work will help you learn and remember the plot of the play. It includes some searching through the play, decision-making, writing down, presentation of your work, and freeze frames.

First divide the class into five groups, which will each work on one Act of the play. You might like to work out your size of groups according to the length of each Act. The grid at the top of page 84 will tell you the number of lines in each Act, and the number of quotes which the group needs to find from that Act.

It would make sense to have a larger group working on Act 3, and a smaller group working on Act 4.

| Act | No. of lines in Act | No. of quotes to find |
| --- | --- | --- |
| Act 1 | 355 lines | 8 quotes |
| Act 2 | 428 lines | 10 quotes |
| Act 3 | 661 lines | 14 quotes |
| Act 4 | 262 lines | 6 quotes |
| Act 5 | 426 lines | 10 quotes |

Then using the list above as a guide, your aim is to find that number of quotes (each up to three lines long) in your Act which will sum up the most important action, events, or thoughts in the Act. Note down your chosen quotes.

## On trial

Several characters in the play have done things they could well be accused of, and even punished for. They are now going to be put on trial and made to account for their actions.

Organize the class as described below.

The five characters on trial each need a defence lawyer or two, s have five groups of three to work on that. One person in each group is the accused.

The prosecution also needs to put its case together, so in addition have five separate pairs. Each pair will prepare together the case against one of the accused.

The whole class should be involved, either in a defence group, c in a prosecution group. When the cases have been prepared, wit supporting evidence from the play in the form of quotations or references, the whole class comes together for the court scene.

For this, one person will be needed for the judge (maybe your teacher) and the rest of the class, when not involved in prosecuting or defending their own case, acts as jury and passes verdicts on the accused.

### Group A

Oberon and Titania are on trial for muddling up the seasons and weather in the mortal world.

### Group B

Egeus is on trial for his harsh treatment of his daughter which resulted in her being exposed to danger, alone, in a forest at night.

### Group C

Puck is on trial for his pranks (ruining the Mechanicals' rehearsal and frightening them) and his mistakes (putting the magic flower juice on the wrong person's eyes).

### Group D

Demetrius is on trial for his fickle and cruel treatment of Helena.

### Group E

Lysander is on trial for his disloyalty to Hermia.


## Horoscopes

None of the characters could possibly have predicted what happens to them in the course of the play: the only certainty at the beginning was that Theseus and Hippolyta would get married four days later, and that they would be celebrating their marriage with 'merriments', 'pomp, triumph, and revelling'.

You probably look at horoscope pages in newspapers or magazines from time to time, so are familiar with the kind of thing they say: it's very general, and usually positive, with only a few hints of difficulties or troubles ahead.

Write the horoscope for one of the lovers or one of the Mechanicals (Bottom is a good example) for the week in which this Midsummer Night falls (in other words, for a week in which 21 June occurs – make up your own dates). Bear in mind what happens in the play, and make your horoscope sound convincing. If your character were to read it at the end of the play, they should be able to recognize clearly that what it foretold did actually come true.

## Language and verse

### Verse

This work on verse can be done in pairs or as a whole class. The two main ideas to grasp about verse, and about the way this play was written, are *rhyme* and *rhythm*. Rhyme is quite easy: all kinds of nursery rhymes and children's songs and game chants rhyme, as you will remember. Rhyme patterns are also easily recognized. Rhythm can be more complex: practise beating out the rhythm in the lines printed below, and also try your hand at other lines from the play.

### *Rhythm*

*A Midsummer Night's Dream* is written in a great variety of verse forms, as well as in prose. The main verse form in the play, as in all Shakespeare's plays, is 'blank verse', or to give it its more formal label, 'iambic pentameter'. This was a very common and conventional way of writing plays during the sixteenth and seventeenth centuries, and most dramatists seem to have preferred it. The iambic pentameter is a five-beat line usually of ten syllables (sometimes an eleventh creeps in) in which the stresses alternate, as in this example:

> The course of true love never did run smooth

(Stresses are marked with the symbol ´ above the syllable to be stressed.)

As you read the lines aloud, beat out the stresses to get the feel of the rhythm.

Blank verse doesn't rhyme. Even so, it is a stylized way of writing, which is still flexible enough to give the illusion of being very close to ordinary speech.

### *Rhyme*

At some points in the play characters speak in a rhyming form of iambic pentameter:

> In that same place thou hast appointed me
> To-morrow truly will I meet with thee.

This kind of two-line rhyme is called a 'couplet'. However, it is worth remembering that couplets can be in any length and rhythm – the label simply means two lines (a couplet) which rhyme.

The speech of many of the characters is neither consistently rhymed nor unrhymed verse but alternates between the two, often in the same speech.

## Other verse forms

You will have noticed that the fairies sometimes speak a verse form with shorter lines, and the songs in the play use a variety of line lengths. Sometimes these lines have two beats, as in:

> Over hill, over dale,
> Thorough bush, thorough brier,
> Over park, over pale,
> Thorough flood, thorough fire

but this pattern then changes immediately into a four-beat line:

> I do wander everywhere,
> Swifter than the moon's sphere . . .

However, you may notice that both the two-beat and the four-beat lines have six (or seven) syllables in the line.

Try to work out how the changed position of the *stresses* in the lines changes the number of *beats* in the lines. You will also notice that this verse rhymes.

## Who speaks what?

Each group of characters in the play speaks in a recognizable, appropriate way. The Elizabethan theatre used minimal props, scenery and 'character' costumes, so language and the ways in which characters spoke were an important way of telling the audience what sort of people the characters were.

■ All the *nobles* speak in blank verse, without exception. Sometimes they also speak in rhymed blank verse.

■ All the *Mechanicals* always speak in prose to each other, or as in Bottom's case, to Titania. However, their play of 'Pyramus and Thisbe', including the prologue spoken by

Quince, is in a variety of verse forms, including the rhyming version of blank verse. (You may remember that they never mention who actually wrote the play, but have got hold of it from somewhere before they start rehearsals.)

■ Of the *fairies*, Oberon and Titania usually speak in blank verse, which sometimes rhymes, but at some points in the play they speak in a different verse form. Puck's speech varies the most of all the characters in the play.

Look back over the play and collect as many examples as you can of different verse forms (rhyming and non-rhyming) and an example of prose.

Can you see any reason why characters who normally speak in unrhyming blank verse should suddenly start to speak in the rhyming version of blank verse? Find a couple of examples of this. Can you spot any sort of pattern?

## Get the rhythm

Below is a speech from the play printed with no punctuation and no line divisions. Copy it out, or have it photocopied, and try to put in the line divisions. If you are successful, try the more difficult task of putting in the punctuation.

good Hermia do not be so bitter with me I evermore did love you Hermia did ever keep your counsels never wronged you save that in love unto Demetrius I told him of your stealth unto this wood he followed you for love I followed him but he hath chid me hence and threaten'd me to strike me spurn me nay to kill me too and now so you will let me quiet go to Athens will I bear my folly back and follow you no further let me go you see how simple and how fond I am

To really 'get the rhythm', try talking to each other in pairs in blank verse: remember to go for ten syllables and five beats. A few examples are:

when I got back from school I had my tea
at school today I had to learn some French
I really understand this Shakespeare play
the hempen homespuns in this play are daft
the fairies spend their time in idle pranks

# Themes and ideas

### Love

In *A Midsummer Night's Dream,* many aspects of the theme of love are explored:

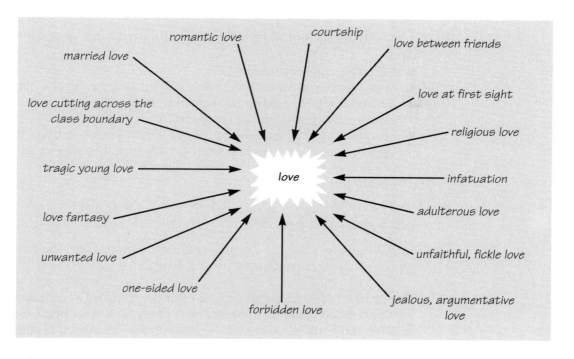

Divide the class into five groups to produce between you a twenty-minute radio or television programme on 'Love in *A Midsummer Night's Dream'*.

Four groups divide the different aspects of love shown in the chart between them.

Each of these four groups plans and produces a three-minute slot on the aspects of love which they have been working on.

These four groups should find and use lines in the play where their aspects of love feature; for example, a group working on unrequited love and infatuation may focus on

- Act 1 scene 1 lines 226–251, when Helena describes how the man she loves, Demetrius, is no longer interested in her
- Act 2 scene 1 lines 188–244 when Helena is, literally, chasing Demetrius through the wood, declaring her love for him – which he rejects.

Each group should mention how the characters they are dealing with behave when they are in love – how the audience knows that they are in love.

The fifth group should provide the continuity for the programme by

- opening the programme
- introducing the theme of love, in all its varieties, in the play
- introducing each group's work and providing a linking commentary with the next group
- concluding the discussion on love. Where possible, this fifth group should also include brief quotes from the play in its own commentary, for example, 'The course of true love never did run smooth.'

## Authority and power

In *A Midsummer Night's Dream*, in both the mortal and the fairy worlds, characters engage in power struggles.

Divide the class into seven groups to fit the number of characters involved. Each group is to present the power relations between the characters listed below in a series of freeze frames or mimes, showing who is in charge or dominant, who is weak or vulnerable, or who is resisting another's power, at these points in *A Midsummer Night's Dream*:

- at the start of the play
- at one or more points as the play develops
- at the end of the play.

Show your freeze frames to the class. Be prepared to be questioned about your thoughts and attitudes by the class.

Each group should look at the relationships within one of these sets of characters:

- Theseus, Hippolyta, and Philostrate
- Egeus, Hermia, and Theseus
- Oberon and Titania

- Quince and the Mechanicals, mainly Bottom
- Puck and the lovers
- Pyramus and Thisbe (and their parents)
- Oberon and Puck.

## Images

Certain key words and images recur in the play. References to love, eyes, night, sleep, dreams, imagination and fantasy, plants and flowers, animals and the natural world run through the text. These words and images work in several ways:

- they build up the play's visual world
- they help create atmosphere
- they express the themes and ideas which the play is concerned with
- they are often closely associated with individual characters.

Divide the class into groups, each of which chooses one of the following groups of images to study:

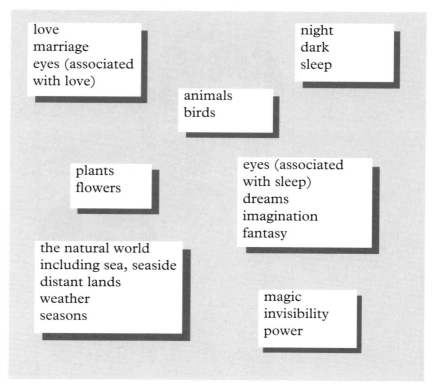

love
marriage
eyes (associated
with love)

night
dark
sleep

animals
birds

plants
flowers

eyes (associated
with sleep)
dreams
imagination
fantasy

the natural world
including sea, seaside
distant lands
weather
seasons

magic
invisibility
power

Collect up as many quotations as you can find referring to your images, and put them together on an image poster. Add the speakers' names and scene references and illustrate your poster with your own drawings or use cut-outs from magazines and other sources.

All the posters can then be displayed together, to give the class a clear and attractive visual impression of the play's images.

## Poster

Look carefully at local posters advertising films, plays, concerts, or other entertainments. Now, produce a poster to advertise a production of *A Midsummer Night's Dream*. Think carefully about:

- one main image from the play which you could present to give an idea of what the play is about, e.g. a blind, winged flying Cupid with his bow and arrow
- the factual information which must be included (e.g. dates) on a poster
- the colours you will use
- any written text to encourage people to attend the performance.

Think about where such posters would be best displayed in your school and neighbourhood. The main audience for your poster is a teenage market.

## Produce a scene

Work in large groups to prepare production notes for a scene, or part of a scene, which you particularly enjoyed. You will probably find about 150–200 lines as much as you can comfortably work on.

You will need to decide first of all on how you wish to present the scene.

There are many possibilities to choose from, but here are some suggestions:

- a modern version, set at some time after 1900
- a period version, set during Shakespeare's own time
- a period version, set in ancient Greece.

When and where you decide to set your version will have an impact not just on costume design, but also on the way your characters behave with each other. It will also convey to the audience certain messages about the play. Professional productions over the years have covered all these ideas, and gone even further. A famous production in 1970 set the play in a futuristic kind of forest, in which the fairies swung about on trapezes, and Puck and Oberon could juggle.

When you have chosen your version, you need to discuss, make notes on, and produce diagrams for all these detailed aspects of a stage production:

- costumes: including any costume changes, wigs, shoes, jewellery
- set: any scenery, backdrop, things on stage like trees, bushes or buildings
- props: objects which characters need during the play, like the flower juice
- music: to accompany the songs, or the dances at the end
- sound: special effects, to enhance the effects you wish to produce, maybe the sounds of the forest at night
- lighting: in this play which takes place largely at night, this is a real challenge
- special effects: technical illusions which you might want to use, like stage fog.

As well as all your production notes, you might like to produce a stage plan, like the one below, to show the set, and where characters should be at one point in your scene:

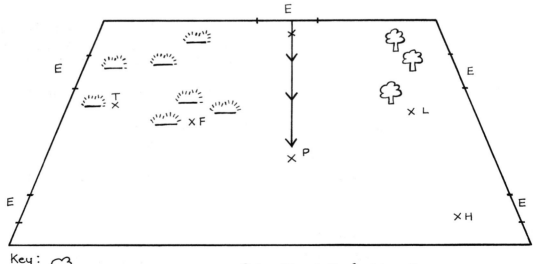

Key:
- Trees
- Bushes
- → → → — Actor moves

Puck : Through the forest have I gone
But Athenian found I none

Before you produce your own stage diagram, work out who the characters are in the one on page 94, and what they are doing.

## Comedy

*A Midsummer Night's Dream* – alongside plays such as *Love's Labours Lost, As You Like It, Much Ado About Nothing,* and *Twelfth Night* – is classed as a comedy. Shakespeare's comedies always feature:

- romance – young people in love – their quarrels, problems and, eventually, marriage
- comic characters or clowns
- a twisted plot full of surprises, sometimes including mistaken identity.

Comedies would usually end with what is called a 'happy ending': young lovers marry, opposed characters are reconciled, the problems posed in the play are somehow resolved. In a tragedy, inevitably, some characters die during or at the end of the play.

However, in *A Midsummer Night's Dream,* there are also moments of tragedy, or near-tragedy.

With a partner, discuss whether *A Midsummer Night's Dream* has all the features of a comedy, and what elements of tragedy you can find in it. Then contribute your ideas to a class discussion.

As you think about the play, consider whether you agree with the following statements:

- everyone in the play has a happy time
- everyone in the play faces problems
- at the end, everyone is happy
- the play within a play, 'Pyramus and Thisbe', is also a comedy.

## Programme

Look carefully at examples of programmes for school, play, ballet, concert, or opera productions. In a small group, produce a theatre programme to accompany a production of *A Midsummer Night's Dream.* Include the following:

- a cover for your programme which hints at what the play is about as well as giving information, for example the venue and times of the performances
- a cast list: either cast the parts from people in your class or famous actors/actresses whom you would choose for the parts
- pictures or photographs (from old programmes)
- appropriate invented advertisements to help to pay for the programme, e.g. for florists/garden centres, a magician/illusionist who entertains at children's parties
- information which you have researched about superstitions and magic in Shakespeare's England.

## Cover

Look carefully at the covers of as many editions of the play as possible. Design a cover for a new edition of *A Midsummer Night's Dream*. Aim to produce a cover which would interest and attract a boy or girl of your own age. Which aspect of the play would you highlight on the cover? For example: young love, magic, a wood on a moonlit night, comedy? Any other aspect?

## Letters and cards

Write Hippolyta's letter to her Amazon people at the end of the play.
Write Lysander's letter to his aunt at the end of the play.
Write Theseus' letter to thank the Mechanicals.
Write a love poem which Lysander could have written for and read to Hermia: 'verses of feigning love' as they were described by her angry father (Act 1 scene 1 line 31).
Write Quince's letter to his actors, thanking them for their hard work and commenting on the way it all went.